GUPP and GOSSIP from the Hills

GUPP and GOSSIP
from the Hills

Ganesh Saili

NIYOGI
BOOKS

Published by
NIYOGI BOOKS
Block D, Building No. 77,
Okhla Industrial Area, Phase-I,
New Delhi-110 020, INDIA
Tel: 91-11-26816301, 26818960
Email: niyogibooks@gmail.com
Website: www.niyogibooksindia.com

Editor: Supriya Mukherjee/Niyogi Books
Design: Arrt Creations

ISBN: 978-93-81523-40-7
Year of Publication: 2012
Reprint: 2018

Printed at Niyogi Offset Pvt Ltd, New Delhi, India

Dedication

For Meera
whose tall tales still resound in my ears.
Sorry Sis! There were no goodbyes this time around!

Contents

Deodar

Introduction

'They sit on their cushions from day to day, with no other amusement than hearing the "gupp-gupp", or gossip of the place'.

MRS SHERWOOD'S AUTOBIOGRAPHY (1809-1810)

I owe this book to the memory of our *Guppastiks* or folks of leisure who've kept the hills busy: some found pleasure in doing; others gossiped. At the very beginning, I confess, this is a very personal collection of *gupp* and gossip from the foothills of the Himalayas.

Rummaging through the dusty drawers of memory, I found these tall tales the town tells. You will find them ephemeral: some full of fun and frolic, others remain, regrettably, tragic.

We have had our fair share of merchants, traders, writers, poets, artists, actors, faith healers and antique dealers. It never ceases to amaze one how quickly in these parts the actual record of events gets confused, how quickly heroes turn into villains and our real history lies buried till it surfaces, albeit briefly, at twilight in family legends. It is no easy task to evoke the past solely from mental notes.

Many years down the road, I share some of this idle prattle and tattle, with you. If you took these folks all together in a single embrace, none of them have ever before been between two covers—literally!

What then do they have in common? You wonder.

All of them, at one point or another have spent time in these hills of Mussoorie where if there's any dirt about, someone or the other is bound to dig it up and leave behind tales to fill up the void.

Such is life for us: everyone knows about everyone's little oddities and eccentricities, those little quirks in our natures, which make us so different yet so special. Though it's a bit like life lived in a fish bowl.

To you, gentle reader I bring these stories full of our scandalous ways, the bonhomie, the skirmishes and reconciliations. None of them are of earth-shattering importance. It's our antics, we do, or say, or think or dream.

Rest assured, very soon there shall be newer tricks to chronicle, dreams to stir, money to bankroll mischief. Yes! This will be another resort with its roguish winners, forgotten losers with unlearned lessons.

But that shall be someone else's *gupp* and gossip for another time.

May both their tribes prosper!

Chapter 1

Of Our Times

Jyun koh bhaisa, aur kitlo koh naag, sayun koh sabla, birala koh bagh

GARHWALI PROVERB

(Lice into buffaloes, and worms into snakes,
needles into crowbars, cats into leopards.)

Those of us, who have spent our lives over a mile up in the sky, have a theory that does the rounds: an outsider who spends too much time here can often seem to be a little touched, and possess a certain cattiness that does not wear off even if they leave to go back to the plains. To know what I mean, there's this letter I found the other day written by a friend of mine, now a whiz kid in the advertising world and who sadly, had to leave us to relocate in Delhi:

> *Dear, Dearest, Darling Ganesh,*
>
> *What's with all the endearments you may well ask? And as you may well have gathered right away, it's my way of saying 'sorry', 'sorrier', and 'sorriest' for turning what may have appeared to be a cold shoulder to your considerate, warm and loving invitation to the hills. It was no cold shoulder, believe me. It was only my depleted state of finances. I should have written to you earlier but you know what a crass, unthinking, uncivilized, uncaring brute I am. I heap these invectives upon myself because I know you must have hurled them at me already. So go ahead, show the 'two fingers' to me if you must and if it helps you vent your steam. I'm ready and waiting to be scalded!*
>
> *And how's the Uttarakhand saga, has it run out of steam or is there an underground movement like the French Resistance and you all go out passing coded messages and what-not like in the movies? What fun playing a cloak-and-dagger routine, running down khuds and hiding messages in hollows of trees! Lest you misunderstand, I'm all for a separate hill state. 'Long Live Uttarakhand!'*
>
> *Is R.B. thrilled with his Padma Shree? Have H & C won awards too for their extensive travelogues? Who are the new authors in town? That place certainly seems to breed writers. Must be something in the water, methinks. I better come and drink at it!*
>
> *Love and fond wishes to everyone at home, including your dogs, Kaali and Bhuri, if they are still around and some baghera hasn't had them for dinner.*

Could it be the lack of oxygen that infuses the mind with a perverse glee? Or is there relief in black humour? Believe me, there's no respite. No one I know has ever got rid of it.

Sometimes, I'm tempted to believe that Lewis Caroll wrote *Alice in Wonderland* with us in mind:

> *'What sort of people live about here?' Alice had asked the Cat. 'In that direction,' the Cat said, waving its right paw round, 'lives a Hatter: and in that direction,' waving the other paw, 'lives a March Hare. Visit either you like: they are both mad.' 'But I don't want to go among mad people,' Alice remarked. 'Oh, you can't help that,' said the Cat: 'We're all mad here. I'm mad. You're mad.'*

Seeing the Slick One, a new-comer twirling around and round the Upper Mall, I casually asked my friend old John Das: 'Is he married? Why does one never see his wife?'

Little did I know that for reasons unknown, he'd taken a dislike to this intruder in our midst. The reply didn't surprise me at all: 'Definitely not!' he exclaimed. 'He's a confirmed bachelor, but then come to think of it, so was his grandfather and his father too. I believe no one's ever got married in their family!'

One could say we are a three-in-one place. There is, first, a place of people like us who were born here or nearby, or came here as small children. We are, all of us without exception, nostalgia buffs who remember the place like it used to be. Yet, we take the place for granted and are guilty of being oblivious to our impressive Himalayan surroundings.

Second, is the town of the men of commerce and professionals—the shopkeepers, the rickshaw pullers, the school teachers and the hoteliers. You shall find that the doctor's clinic you saw last year is now a shoe shop, while the public urinal is today's *dhaba* (eatery), the chemist is selling hamburgers and the look-out point has sprouted a motor-cycle repair shop.

'There's so much money here,' complains my friend Prof Sudhakar Misra, 'that bookshops are now selling suitcases!'

Yes! They all have an eye on the cash register, were born elsewhere and came to the hill station in search of a job, or a business opportunity, or are looking for a small dream cottage with a tuft of grass to step out on.

Third, are the tourists who fill up the place for without them the economy would crash. They turn the town upside down, and it doesn't matter whether it's your yuppie from Chandigarh or Panipat on holiday or honeymoon, or a girl who has run away from home, or a gaggle of wide-eyed school children on an excursion. It makes no difference. They keep the money flowing.

In 1888, a correspondent observed: 'Mussoorie is the cheapest hill station; hotels are good. Society rather mixed, houses rent cheaply, and provisions also; but the distances from the bazaar are great, and many people allow their cook a pony… A large number of retired officers, reside in the valley during winter, come up for summer where educational advantages are good.'

Education is the last thing on the mind of the summer hordes who arrive to play out their personal fantasies. When you see Mrs Blubber, the Aunty*ji*-types from Karolbagh in see-through negligees, cavorting on the Mall, dipping *jalebis* in *doodh* at the *halwai's* shop, please be tolerant. The poor thing has already spent four hours at the beauty parlour just getting an estimate. After all the servicing, the denting-painting, it doesn't help when on her return the husband asks: 'What happened? Was the parlour closed again today?' Unkind cut that, if you realise, she's been there for the better part of the day. Though it's not going to get her anywhere in this uneven contest with Mrs Slim, her own daughter-in-law.

Yes! That's what she wants to do. It's her thing! Please let her be.

Let's not lament the days sieved by when the Mall—our main promenade—in the evening was the general resort of everyone. An old newspaper clipping I found proclaims: 'Where every conceivable variety of hat, bonnet, shawl, waistcoat, petticoat and pantaloon, was seen, jumbled up together in one grand masquerade. The chief amusement of this gay spot consists of elaborate and busy idleness in which archery, picnics and balls suffice for the gentler sex; whilst billiards, brandy and betting keep the men going.'

All that has changed. Nowadays, if you meet anyone in formal attire, there's a good chance they are on their way to a funeral, a housewarming or a wedding.

Come summer and our limited eateries are woefully inadequate to cater to the twenty lakh or more tourists who gridlock the place.

How do we feed them?

Street-vendors convert defunct phone booths into shacks, crammed shoulder to shoulder along the roadsides, offering: steamed corn-on-the-cob, chow mein, *bhel-puri, chaat,* boiled eggs, *pau-bhaji* and momos.

Above the shanties rise rows of newer hotels built matchbox style with poky little rooms. Chances are, the visitor who arrives here after sunset, may well find themselves lodged in a cramped little room with wall to wall beds, where the furniture has been painted on the walls and outside the window rises an orange plastic palm-tree standing like a long lost bookmark!

I was witness to this irate outburst from a customer at the Shapira hotel: 'Look, do you think I'm an idiot or what? I booked a double-room, not this tiny cell with a stool.'

'But this is not your room, sir, this *is* the lift.'

Lifting the soul is the prospect that one can, if one so desires, behave in ways that maybe considered improper elsewhere or are frowned upon in other places. Our unwritten code often provokes risqué or unconventional conduct.

'Here! Call your parents! Tell them where you are!' snap the policemen at the half-way toll barrier, thrusting a cell phone in the face of the young couple playing truant from college astride a flashy bike.

It never works. Every now and then a scandal occurs, which makes the moralists lift the whites of their eyes and thank Heaven they are not such sinners as that. 'There is not such a place as these hills for the tongue of false report to wag about,' wrote a visitor in the 1920s. Even now, everybody thinks everybody else's affairs to be more worth looking after than their own.' If you have a friend or two to lunch, tea or dinner, the whole town is sure to know before noon next day what was on your table and who said or ate what.

For instance, last winter, at the first sign of snow, my phone began to ring incessantly.

'Uncle*ji*! Has it snowed up there?' a complete stranger from Dehra asked me.

I barely had to nod. By the time I put the phone down trouble was scurrying up the hill. Crowds of revellers arrived to enjoy the season's first snowfall. Barely had the Belham's schoolgirls got down at the bus-stand, they were greeted by a reception committee pelting them with snowballs.

The matter could not to be taken lightly. It was a matter of great concern. The inquisition began on their return. 'Next time!' suggested the stern Principal, '...we could send the Goon School boys as chaperones!'

Loud peals of laughter almost brought down the roof of the school auditorium. Known for many other things, pampered Goscos are not exactly famous for their chivalry.

'Congratulations!' I heard the young Mrs Robust exclaim on seeing her friend Mrs Luscious, looking gloriously pregnant waddling down the bazaar. When she complained: 'We've been trying for years—but no such luck so far!'

'Well, why don't you do what I did,' said Mrs Luscious, adding in a whisper: 'Go to the faith healer in Barlowganj. But do go on your own.'

Many people who went to school here return to the scene of the crime, as it were to discover that things have changed. For instance, an old friend of mine, Angela Middleton, who was a student at the austere, vegetarian Seventh Day Adventist School in the 1930s, tells me: 'They relied as little as possible on hired labour with the students doing all the manual work.'

'Now don't you go eating chilly pickle!' the grumpy matron used to warn the girls as they went out to town: 'It *heats* the blood!'

'The moment we hit town, we gobbled up as much of it as we could. Alas! No miracles happened,' Angela chuckles almost sixty years later.

'Still waiting for it to *heat* the blood!' she jokes.

In our hot bed of flirtations, if Jack does come up the hill, it's usually with someone else's Jill. Only those wet behind the ears will believe they have come to fetch a pail of water. Up here, Cupid is always at play and many couples find bliss at the numerous wedding points in town. Luckily, at least, for the owners of these places, there are more honourable weddings than scandalous elopements.

'We've been sustained by our commentators,' Mrs Chatpatti, our spice expert tells me while adding a dollop of chillies to her tone.

Take our two old biddies Mrs Gupp and Mrs Gossip—don't you be taken in by their woebegone looks; one is the *The Happy Valley Express*, while the other is a local edition of *The Times of the Hills*! Deftly, with precision, the two have carved up their territory and continue to exchange notes. Make no mistake, they are prosecutor, jury, judge and executioner, all rolled into one. Its non-stop: 'Breaking News' 24x7. If it's not about some maharajah (yes! a few still survive), it's the mayhem in a school, or a Principal's mistress, or the pleasures of landed gentry taking to drink, consumed with unrequited love for their neighbour's wife.

'How I wish we knew some of the people Mrs Gupp gossips about!' complained Mrs Gossip. True! The moment she meets you, she'll whisper in your ear about folks you have never heard of or will ever hear of again.

At the top, surrounded by a fine canopy of hill oaks, rhododendrons, deodars and a fine strawberry patch is the Parsonage, a bird watcher's paradise. This is home to thespian Victor Banerjee. On a quiet day, you shall find him with a pair of binoculars in hand, more than happy to help distinguish the Red-billed blue magpie from its cousin, the Black-throated jay. He doesn't like the rude crows and shoos the intruders as they flap in from the nearby army Mess, with desiccated kitchen scraps in their beaks to moisten in his bird bath.

'They mess the water!' he moans.

Many years ago, as luck would have it, Mrs Sheila Bhate, his mother-in-law was visiting, to keep her daughter, the beautiful Maya, company while our actor hared off for a film shoot. Now, mother-in-law did not approve of sharing the strawberries with the birds. Stumbling upon an ancient, crumbling, moth-eaten apology of a panther skin in the study, she planted it in the middle of the garden like a scarecrow to frighten away the avian intruders.

Scare them?

Yes she did—out of a year's growth!

Trouble was the skittish birds left the fruit, left the garden and abandoned the locality not to return. A full month after he came back from work, Victor shook his head in disbelief. He failed to join the dots as he sat there gloomily, with the binoculars and bird books beside him for hours on end, scratching his head, puzzled as to where the birds had vanished.

The bad news was that Maya and mother-in-law were not telling.

Nor was I. Sworn to secrecy my lips were sealed!

It was a full six months or so later that the birds forgave and forgot and returned to gambol in the bird bath once again.

Though there was nothing skittish about our royalty here. At the turn of the nineteenth century, this outcrop of the Himalayas became the prime choice for the Indian princes. Foremost among these were, the Maharajah of Kapurthala, who built the exotic Chateau de Kapurthala, and the Ranas of Nepal, whose Fairlawn Palace lies sprawled across a ridge in Jharipani.

Thrown into this cauldron were the celebrated exiles: Dost Mohammed and his son Akbar Khan, exiled in Balahissar in the summer of 1841; Yakub Khan, an ex-Amir of Afghanistan, interned at Bellevue, and Maharajah Dalip Singh, son of legendary Maharajah Ranjit Singh, the Lion of Punjab, who was tucked away in the Castle Hill Estate, while the British robbed him of his kingdom.

Other rulers too like Patiala, Bhopal, Rajpipala, Nabha, Panna, Baroda and Jind, built themselves splendid homes and in their wake came Tikari, Cooch Behar, Palanpur, Kasmanda, Kateswar, Rampur and Indore.

Who would dare match the fun and frolic at Chateau de Kapurthala with its fancy dress balls soaked in fire-water; where tables creaked with copious amounts of food as guests abandoned their scruples and we are told: 'Some bold women did not hesitate to take their lovers to their houses to share their bed.'

Those days of wine and song, made it a place of gaiety, frivolity and sexual indulgence. Though personally, I have no faith in the wag who said: 'One drink you were happy. Two—drunk. Three you were under the table, and four you were likely to be under the host!'

This summer, when I drop by the quiet grounds of the imposing Chateau de Kapurthala, I saw a congress of black-faced langurs hold court in the gardens. I was there to catch up with the present guardian, the venerable HH Brig Sukhjit Singh. He had just settled down for a sun-downer on the veranda. Just as the bearer brought him his favourite whiskey-soda-ice, his phone rang. He stepped inside to take the call. When he got back, his drink was missing. Looking up, he saw a langur perched on the railings of the first floor balcony, flicking his tail in appreciation.

Is there anything better than the aroma of a good peaty malt to start one's evening?

To such a witches' brew came my father Mukand Ram Saili, a strapping lad from a remote village in the border district of Chamoli-Garhwal, looking for *any* job. He was just another number, a statistic in the male exodus from the hills in search of livelihood. His first incarnation saw him as a meter-reader with the electricity department. It entailed wandering from lane to lane, house to house, bungalow to bungalow, jotting down digits. I can still hear him regale us with close encounters of a special kind with the quirky residents of those big houses with high gates. Into the alien world of fancy hotels like the Savoy, Hakman's and Charleville, he went and saw bearers in white uniforms with maroon cummerbunds and gold sashes and tassels flitting between tables in the ballrooms. The glamour, the clothes, the spit and polish of these places with mounted trophies on the walls, must have been such a far cry from the realities of his humble abode in Sail village.

Tales of his wanderings, not from country to country, but from lane to street, hovel to house, shack to bungalow—each a planet unto itself—brought home a host of characters who were to people my imagination forever.

Years down the road, in the 1970s, a rainbow of colourful flower-children were to change the face of the hillside. Living like gypsies, you could say it was a 'far-out' phase—just a wee bit *too* over the edge!

'We are all about peace, harmony, happiness, love and compassion!' Mr Raffish, a sixty-something year old hippie assured me.

Where shall I begin this Ginsberg phase?

Maybe with the Frenchman Pierre's psychedelic shoes, one pink and the other blue; follow it up with Fat Mary's penchant for wrapping herself in a burqa to avoid roving eyes in her walks through the bazaar; or Blind George who could recognise you by your voice as he straddled the globe with the prettiest femme fatales nuzzling him along; Michael, our 'Hatman' from Down Under with a hustle of rakish Akubra hats, lit up the hillside, almost putting it out of joint; or Raymond Louis Steiner of Baton Rouge, Louisiana who became the new age Guru; or Gila, the Flying Dutch lady whose affair with natural fabric dyeing blessed her with four children, each with a different surname; Abu and Lakshmi Tripathi, whose triplets arrived just in time to upset the family planning programme; or Hans, the Swiss handy man, and Ram Alexander, the Texan, reputedly an oil tycoon who dropped his jeans, grew his hair, went ethnic to flee to an ashram in Rishikesh to learn Zen Buddhism mixed with tantric sex.

Add a pinch of weed, throw in the strains of Rastafarian vibrations and you almost had a mini-Goa up here. The gradual tightening of liberal visas ended those smoke-filled pipe dreams of the 1970s.

At first glance, you'll be tempted to think of us ragamuffins as flippant. Does it all date back to our founding fathers that were in the employ of the not-so-honourable John Company? For example, the town's founder, if you'd like to call him that, Col Young, who we are told was an honest, upright officer. Or was he? How did he come to acquire a 16,000 acre farm in Dehra?

And he was not alone in the plunder. Later arrivals were greedier. Col (later Sir) George Everest arrived in the winter of 1832 and bought the 283 acre Park Estate which was fair enough had it ended there, but soon after he had logged 640 acres. Could this have been done without diddling the unlettered headman of Rikholi village? Of course there are no land records and the unwritten commandment forbids judging with hindsight.

But the more things change, the more they remain the same. Whoever broods over the past sees that many things were much as they are now. So, even now, the tradition continues in the mysterious disappearance of trust properties. Could it be that sometimes, the fence gets really hungry and ends up swallowing the field? For instance, in one of our charitable hospitals, Mr Sleaze, the business manager was delegated the delicate task of getting custom clearance in Mumbai for an x-ray machine, donated by a well-meaning Baptist Mission. Apparently, all went well till in the spirit of free enterprise, he flogged the equipment in Chor Bazaar, resigned from the job to set himself up as an upright businessman in one of the new shopping malls in the Doon. You're right! We never saw him again in the hills. If you dare mention his name in missionary circles, they break out in hives.

Dr Crafty, another leading light of the community sold to himself an entire bungalow owned by the trust he happened to head. Trouble came knocking when he decamped with all the surgical instruments from the operation theatre to set himself a neat little medical practice, which too shut down—after his affair with a ward-boy did not go down too well with one of the stretcher-bearers!

Vulnerable to white-collar crimes are educational trusts, where some of the old orphanages have been turned into five-star resorts. Yes! Charity begins at home. Though you could say in favour of a certain Mr Schemer, a poacher turned gamekeeper, that the school had been his wife, his children, and his home; his one long and lasting passion. And he was content that it had been so. He had no regrets for missed opportunities elsewhere.

'I will continue to live in Pine Spur cottage,' he announced to the wide-eyed Board of Directors, and before they could as much as catch their breath, he delivered the coup de grace: '... for the rest of my life!'

Language Block.

Believe me, he's still there. Principal and Chairman for five years, he's lived gratis for twenty-five years. And, to me, it looks like he's in no hurry to go anywhere.

The school did try to wedge the old man out. They lost. Who can teach a mad man the name of his father?

'Always do something. Don't ever just sit around!' the late Cecil Garlah, my kindergarten teacher used to tell me. Little surprise then that no one batted an eyelid when one of the school's more gifted clerks, Mr Gheese champing at the bit, just before his retirement to palm fringed Kerala, fudged the minutes of the last board meeting, gifting himself a lovely ivy-draped cottage on the fringes of the school before promptly selling it to the highest bidder and vanished. 'Mission Impossible' accomplished in a week flat!

Chapter 2

Monkey Trouble

Cwapugun khane madu thaya conpin manuta biswas madu

NEPALI PROVERB

(Those who live in a place from where the Himalayas cannot be seen may not be trusted.)

At the time of writing, the monkey menace is a lightning rod for a great deal of public anger in the hills. Everyone seems to be perpetually persecuted by them. At the old Charleville, guards armed with airguns stalk the campus to scare off the simians, especially after one of the aggressive rhesus monkeys lunged at one of the Deputy Directors, completely disregarding his seniority, forcing him to take immediate evasive action. He jumped over the railing straight into the defile down below. Result? A broken arm!

Or you could say that Mr Obtuse, a college professor was to a certain extent responsible for the sudden explosion in the rhesus population. Don't jump the gun and get me wrong. It all goes back to the winter vacation when our dear teacher went off to his home in the plains.

On meeting an old friend, he jokingly complained of a flagging libido. 'I'll fix that!' promised the friend. Later, he gave him some specially concocted sweetmeats put together by a renowned herbalist, who'd made a minor fortune peddling cures for all kinds of sexual ailments, near the Clock Tower in Moradabad.

Fortified with a box brimming with aphrodisiacs, our professor came home to his flat in the narrow lanes of our bazaar. On the very first day, he ate one, leaving the box near the window. The rest, as they say, is history—not his, theirs!

A pesky monkey grabbed the box, spilling the contents on the ledge below. In the ensuing free for all, the sweets were gobbled up by a troupe of monkeys. Now don't ask me if it worked. Honestly! I don't know. But you have my word for it—there was an immediate jump in the population of

simians. I hear there were rumours that one of these red-bottomed rhesus' had a big grin on his face whenever he peeped through the barred windows of the learned professor's abode looking for fresh supplies!

And grinning were the langurs too at one of the town's best walkers, a certain Miss Crabbit who, having retired from a girl's school settled here and has not stopped walking since. Given to the belief that those who walk sixteen kilometres a day are blessed with an eternal life, she sets off on her walk after a frugal breakfast, returns home for lunch, and takes off again to stagger home at dusk.

Things went well for years, that is until one of her nieces brought her a silvery fur coat to keep her warm through the cold winter. Hardly had she stepped out of her flat, when she noticed that she was being trailed by a troupe of amorous black-faced langurs marching in step behind her!

Now! That's *real* monkey business.

Up until the 1960s, we had a tradition of doctors who made their way to the mountains from the sultry Ganges delta of Bengal. Foremost among these was a Dr Mitra, who ran a private clinic near the Old Theatre. On retiring, he passed on his practice to Dr Bagchi who, for some weird reason, always wore a monkey-cap. You could tell that summer had come when the good doctor removed his cap and little kids on the road went around yelling: *'Papu ki topi uttar gayey!'* (Old man's taken off his cap!)

Dr Bhaduri though had no cap fetish, he specialized in sex problems. Right next to the Electric Picture Palace cinema, he had a garish hoarding that showed an exhausted lion lying flat on its face before imbibing his magical aphrodisiac, while on the other side there was that magnificent pride of Africa, roaring at the tourists much in the manner of the MGM lion. Things were going well for the good doctor, up until the day police came knocking at his door.

What could he have done? He wondered. His medicines were not *that* bad!

The warrant stated he had certified as dead a man who was alive and kicking, and mad and angry too, because meanwhile his estranged wife had run off with the proceeds of his insurance policy. Off to the police station they marched and into the lock up he went for the night. The barred metal door clanged shut only to be opened the next morning when he was produced before a magistrate.

Lo and behold! As luck would have it, the doctor recognised Mr Tormented, the duty magistrate, as the errant youth whom he had a long time ago treated for venereal disease. Now, seated on his august chair, memories of another day came flooding back, he could still remember the burning sensation every time he had to visit the loo. Bashfully, he now remembered approaching the doctor, and managed to mutter: ‘Doctor Sa’ab, I think my thing has a cold.’

Dr Bhaduri had taken one look, smiled and said: ‘Till it sneezes, may be I’ll treat you with penicillin.’

On this fated day, their eyes met again. Time's relentless sand papering had weathered them both as the clock rewound to twenty years ago. What mattered was that at the decisive moment, they were partners in crime again.

'Doctor Sa'ab! What are you doing *here*?' asked the judge.

'Police say I've certified the living as dead! And his wife has taken off with his insurance!'

'How did that happen?'

'These men dragged me out of my bed at night and into a hotel room,' he recalled, almost as in a dream. 'Yes! There was a body. I wrote the name they gave me. Can you ask a dead man his name?'

'True! Very possible!' nodded Tormented, saying: 'A case of mistaken identity. Bail granted.'

For the rest of his days, I am told Dr Bhaduri stopped taking house calls. The word was out that he would break out in hives if you so much as

Doctor's Clinic

phoned him to take a house call. He changed track, as it were and switched to breeding dogs. And that went quite well, as things usually do, till he used some cheap hair-dye on his white Pomeranians to turn them into Samoyeds.

Though, not a shadow of doubt lingered near our school's physician, Dr Stutter who unwittingly, opened our mind to forbidden fruit. He was a quiet man, the kind of person who could go through life without a trace of adventure. In line with school policy, once every three months, he would give us a physical examination. Off we were marched, single-file, like a chain-gang, one for the boys and one for the girls, up to the school's crumbling dispensary, perched atop an eyrie on the cliff.

There stood the greying doctor bolstered by his assistant, the chubby nurse, whom we called 'Big Boobs'. If you peeped at the girl's section, all one saw popping up were the girls' hands from behind a green screen. Had it not been for the austere surroundings, you'd wonder if a bank robbery was in progress and the hooded robbers had yelled: 'Hands up!'

Dr Stutter was checking the girls for tell-tale lumps. Of course, the boys were easier to deal with or so one would have thought! He would point at our fly and say: 'Take it out! Take it out!' If it wasn't squeaky clean, he would turn his nose up in disgust, drop your thing and say loud and clear: 'Waashit!' Dipping his hands in a washbasin, he would repeat almost to himself: 'Waashit!'

Down the years, his name was forgotten. It was erased from our juvenile minds. But if you should meet an ex-student from the 1960s, you could make instant friends by simply yelling: Waashit!

One day, Big Boobs complained to Waashit that some fresher from Thailand ate beetles. Waashit paused. His face grew grave, very troubled.

'Betels! Now what's wrong with that?' Waashit looked puzzled adding: 'Where I grew up in Lucknow, everyone ate *paan*!'

'Oh! Doctor! Not those!' muttered the nurse, explaining: 'These ones fly around!'

'Oh! Why didn't you say so the first time?'

Waashit nibbled at his bleached nails and said almost to himself: 'Now we've got a problem!'

In the traumatic days after partition, legend has it that a trainload of refugees from the troubled North West Frontier Province headed to Saharanpur, arrived there too late at night, slept through the journey and found themselves deposited on the rail terminus in Dehra. This marked their entry into the valley where in their resettlement, or so we are told, they were ably assisted among others by Rai Bahadur Capt Kirparam, the first Indian owner of the legendary Savoy hotel. Other fresh entrants from the cooler climes of Bannu or Muree, made their way up the hill to be born again as dry fruit merchants, vegetable sellers and drapers. The enterprising ones, dressed up in salwar kameez became mendicants and took to selling pavement concoctions.

Like an able apothecary, one such entrepreneur would spread a sparkling white sheet on the roadside, open a tin truck, lay out his wares, and sure enough a large crowd of curious folks would gather very soon around him.

'Those who can't perform in bed or whose thing is stuck like a clock at six-thirty, wake up! Try *Shilajit*—the king of all medicines. I have brought it all the way from the mountain tops of Kandahar!'

'*Imam-jasta*! Mortar and pestle! Wouldn't you like to go home, stiff like a pestle? Your virility so hard, that if you strike a stone, it will crack and if you hit an electric pole, it'll sound like a school bell. And the students will think school is over!' Peals of laughter welcomed such irreverent rendition of the plain facts of life.

A movement distracts him. A curious old lady hobbles through the crowd to see what's on sale. He takes this in his stride, yelling: 'Old woman!

There's nothing for you here. Go home. Your old man must be panting for you!'

And the fable careens on: 'Once upon a time there was a king who ate *jharmakra* (a herbal concoction!)—he kept going till mid-night—next morning he was still *tagra* (strong)!'

Deftly he pours a few drops of glycerine over a thimble full of permanganate crystals. The resultant fumes set the crowd's imagination afire. This is pure magic! No stopping his unstoppering a bottle, taking out a few drops of pinkish oil, declaiming: 'This is *sanday-ka-tel* (lizard oil)! One drop is enough to make your manhood stiff as the Clock Tower!'

But he was only just warming up: 'On honeymoon, a man spent the entire night, right up to the break of dawn, sitting up staring at his beautiful bride.'

'What've you been thinking?' she finally asked.

'I've been thinking,' said the hulk, 'How *khoobsurat* (good looking) your brother must be!'

More mirth and laughter!

In autumn, each mohalla, both big or small, organised their own Ram Lilas. My favourite was enacted on a flat above the bazaar where the dialogues were laced with a distinct Pashto lilt.

In one poignant scene, Hanuman's army mounts an attack on Lanka, to free Sita from the clutches of Ravana, the Demon king. Little boys dressed up to swell the ranks of the monkey army. Hanuman clad in a glittering *kulla* (turban), gold shining through the *turra* (coxcomb), came sliding down an improvised ropeway. All went well, that is, until the support wire snapped and he came crashing down on to the stage. Predictably, pandemonium reigned. In the flush of battle, the boys in excitement whipped out their toy pistols (oblivious of the fact that such modern weaponry did not exist in the days of the Ramayana) and pressed the trigger. Bang! Bang! Smoke billowed on the stage. The audience cracked up, convulsed in laughter.

Perhaps it was a sign of times to come, of life imitating folklore. One thing was for sure—the culture of the gun had arrived in the sleepy backwaters of the valley down below.

Among our many 'firsts' was the opening of the first post office in 1827. The empire builders ensured that mail was accessible to the troops convalescing here.

How we take the postman who delivers letters to our doorstep for granted. It was not always so. Two hundred years ago, the job of mail runner was a risky one, and the *hikara* as he was called, had to seek protection with a spear or sword. After dark, these brave runners assisted by torchbearers, went through our forests accompanied by *dug-duggiwalas* (tom-tom boys) to keep wild animals at bay.

On the prowl were man-eating tigers and leopards. An old guide tells me that in 1810, the countryside was so infested with predators that the roads were almost impassable. Day after day, for nearly a fortnight, some of the *dak* people were carried off, at one or the other passes, by tigers.

Our last mail-runner in the 1970s, was a simple-minded fellow called Teju, perhaps the only person they could find willing to carry the mail to Suakholi, along the road to Tehri, a distance of six miles for a measly five rupees a day. This he did every day for thirty years! Maybe it was not about money at all. That was not what he was looking for.

A short, non-descript man of easy demeanour, he was grumpy but loyal and went about his chosen task, swaddled like a gollywog, wrapped up in a pile of clothes. He had no family, no friends, never took care of his appearance and was generally, ill-kempt. Living like a turtle, carrying all his earthly possessions on his back, he went through life adding, vest upon vest, shirt upon shirt, coat upon coat and topping it all off with a grand final gesture—

an old dressing gown of uncertain vintage, frayed at the edges. A friend put it: 'Teju is always lost in his wardrobe!'

The last memory I have of him is struggling to get into a new set of clothes with annoyance, surprise and concern! It was certainly one of these feelings that flitted across his face as he sighed: 'These trousers are a bit *too* tight in the armpits!'

Late one afternoon, quietly, as was his manner, without any fuss, he left for the Great Beyond. They found his remains, curled up, under the outdoor counter of the post office. The entire bazaar gathered for the cremation at the bottom of the hill. The crush was dense, the day already warm, and would have been hotter, but for the light zephyr that stirred among the long leafed pine on the hillside; it was as if the Gods wished to give him a fitting welcome on his return.

Personally, I think Teju would have appreciated the breeze. In life, or in death, he would not have had anyone uncomfortable on his account.

Another life and death thing is our local elections which were marked by moments of levity. Who can deny that certain parts of the town are tawdry, others are downright wretched, and just becoming worse with advancing age. Cynical as it may sound, we seem to get the government we deserve. Long before the Election Commission stepped in to tighten the screws, our local hopefuls used every trick in the book to inveigle the voters in the 1960s.

Take Balbir Singh, the vegetable seller, who offered himself as a candidate in the election. Amidst the dust and din on polling day, the aroma of food drew everyone to his bedecked counter where beaming from ear to ear, brimming with confidence, he whispered: 'Three hundred and forty two people have already had lunch here!'

Our soothsayer predicted: 'All good lunches don't always convert into good votes!'

Surprise! Surprise! On counting day, he got only thirty-four votes!

Elsewhere, one missing vote led to bad blood in one of our old families. A local general merchant, Fatso, the grand old patriarch with a large joint family of twenty folks, polled only nineteen votes. The dogs of war were about. Who was the treacherous one in the ranks? It plagued the family for a long time. And all the solemn oaths taken with holy Ganga-water, and basil leaves, and a row of small metal urns full of salt, never did clear up the clouds over that single missing vote!

Another missing vote led to bad blood between two close friends, the Wheezer and the Greazer, both of whom were elected councillors, but parted ways over the rampant horse-trading for the coveted post of the Chairman. Things went out of hand, as it were when Greazer used his casting vote against Wheezer. As the winner, bowed down with garlands big enough to have bent the Bamiyan Buddha, went past the other—our vanquished hero, the Wheezer, hired a loudspeaker from the local tent house, pointed it in the direction of his old friend's house, and played all day long at full blast a popular song from a movie of the 1960s:

Ehsaan meray dil pey tumhara hai doston,
Yeh dil tumharay pyar ka maara hai doston!
('You've done such a favour to my heart, friends...
This heart is shattered by the kindness of friends like you!')

Shattered was the anxious spouse, the Worrier, of one of our electoral hopefuls for during campaigning, he took to standing on crossroads buttonholing all and sundry. Mass contact was, he believed, the trick to win friends and influence enemies.

'Are you from Ward Number B?' he'd buttonhole teenage boys going home at dusk.

'Yes, we are,' they'd say.

'Here! Take this chit, go to the booze shop near Shapira hotel, pick up your bottle and have a great evening!'

And so they did to stagger home in various stages of inebriation. It was the parents who were not amused.

Nor was the Worrier. As a result of her husband's enthusiasm, she lost her first election.

'Next election,' she told her husband, in a voice as dry as bone, 'if you really want me to win, pack your bags and leave for your home in the village two months before the election!'

That's exactly what he did five years later. Result? The Worrier won!

Though one of our *thekedars* or contractors (our town is full of them) refused to pack up and leave. He carried a voter's list in hand, crossing off the names of all those who definitely were *not* going to vote for him. He did it openly. Soon every voter saw that the crosses outnumbered the ticks. And your guess is as right as mine! He lost.

'Nothing worse than an out-of-work politician,' a local scribe told me. 'He'll never put his hands in his pockets even when it's cold!'

Yes! Local elections are serious affairs. If you go by the old records, in 1934, a senior citizen who stood for election, died of heart failure soon after the counting was over. The shock of winning proved too much for him.

There is no love lost in the din of an election campaign. I believe that the easiest way of tracing one's ancestry, distant and immediate, is to stand for any public office in a small town.

'Aristocrat? My foot!' urged a friend talking of the cherubic Mr Suri, staring down from a bunting: 'Don't you get taken in by that dinner jacket and bow tie. He started life at a cycle-puncture repair shop!'

Elsewhere, at the butt end of the populace's ire, a newly elected councillor picked up the phone to hear a shrill voice scream: 'Rukum Ram! One has to light a match to see the puddle of light from the street lamp outside my gate!' It was our *The Times of the Hills* on the line.

'What you saying madam?' he shilly-shallied.

'Why? You got pebbles in your mouth! Just put a bigger light bulb!'

'Just now coming madam!' he jabbered, gingerly placing the phone back into its cradle, frightened that she might worm her way through the phone lines into his home.

'Crazy chap!' she said to me. 'Looks like Death warmed up,' adding: 'With a face only his mother would like, how on earth did he win an election?'

'Last time when I told him that something must be done for the uplift of the middle class; he gave me a withering look and said: "Middle Class? I have always done so much for the middle classes... I loved it so much in school that I spent three years between class five and six!"'

Chapter 3

Man-Eaters In The Hills

Khontu say khulyun gooru kooda hey khandoh
GARHWALI PROVERB

(A cow set free from its stake only eats garbage.)

Believe it or not, this place was always a station for scandals. Yet one secret it has kept to itself is the tale of its own man-eaters. It is a *shikar* story of sorts, but these predators were so lethal that even Jim Corbett, would not have dared pursue, stalk, or attempt to bring them down.

Now don't you go haring off into the nearby forests looking for them. They live amongst us and their depredations could put to shame any self-respecting leopard that prowled these hills. Our man-eaters are wilier, craftier and more cunning than that dreaded king of Rudraprayag, who, according to government records, was the 'best-hated and most feared feline', and logged 125 kills in the 1920's.

What protects them? A conspiracy of silence which throws a gossamer veil of secrecy over their depredations.

Take Aunty*ji*—for that is what the whole town would soon come to call Mrs Horny. A Shankhani, jumped out of the pages of the *Kama Sutra*, Vatsyana's dream woman. Her daintiness, her pretty skirt, her good looks and stocky charm helped her find employment as a maid with a retired magistrate. Confronted by her alabaster skin, ebony hair, slanting eyes, pouting lips and full figure—what chance did the old man stand? Seduced? He was left in knots, tongue-tied, hit by lightning which erased all memories of his family in the plains, as he moved into a little cottage, fathering three children before finally moving on to the Happy Hunting grounds.

If you thought that was the end of the story, you have a thing or two coming. If you looked closely at Mrs Horny, she seemed like a woman of forty, or perhaps a year or two more. On the other hand, she might be a year or two less. She had the figure of a nymph, and though her head was flecked with grey, it could not be taken as a sign of age.

It seemed as if trouble had been no stranger to her. There were little tell-tale lines about the eyes, which told their own tale, and though the face smiled pleasantly, one could see she was lonely. A fatal condition that's certainly not hard to remedy here as there never was a dearth of little Jack Horners. They came, they succumbed, and were conquered, ravished and devoured.

Only the town's old biddies shook their heads as they looked down their noses to say: 'Only piece of cutlery the poor thing knows is a teaspoon!'

'She's a jag-juicer!' Mr Fikar, one of our grey heads remarked, explaining: 'A sugarcane press. Once the cane is in, you can't pull it out. It has to come out at the other end with all the juice squeezed out!'

When the lovers were done with, they were discarded. What use is chaff after the grain has been threshed?

And hardly anyone, in the beginning at least saw the evil lurking in those sparkling eyes. It brought to mind old stories of ancient people who sap the vigour of younger ones to replenish their own.

'When all that's stiff are his socks—take the money and run!' was her simple rule of the thumb. Her victims included Mr Randy, a lean, balding professor who lived in the neighbourhood, not too far from her home. One monsoon day he found himself, as was his wont, having supper with Mrs Horny. In the torrential rain, they decided it would be best to spend the night together. Our hills lend themselves to such happy thoughts, feeding and encouraging them.

On this stormy night, their lovemaking spilled over well into dawn. The world seemed to be going too well for the professor that night. Almost perfect! That is, till there was a knock on the door. Calamity had come unannounced. At first, they ignored it. For a space of time, the two love-makers lay supine in the darkness, and both listened intently. The knocking was insistent. Someone stirred outside the door. Understandably, they were not too pleased. Aunty*ji*'s gifted hands had just begun the Hopping of the Hare, tweaking the old man's flaccid nipples and had just about managed to arouse his flagging manhood for one last encore.

'Who's there?' yelled Mrs Horny.

'Mum! It's me—*Mottu*!'

Aunty*ji*'s doting son, had on an impulse, boarded the overnight bus from Delhi (where he was studying) and surprised everyone. That was the kind of person he had always been—a specialist at being in the wrong place at the right time.

Silently, she tiptoed towards the door just as our professor in the nude, clothes under his arms, bolted from the room through the back door, down the wooden staircase of the service entrance and skidded on a slippery plank! Fortunately, the sound of the ensuing thud was drowned out by the tattoo of the rain on the tin roof. Shrugging his shoulders in post-coital lethargy, he limped through the rain thinking: 'It'll be alright so long as a student doesn't see me with my pants down.' Mr Randy was aware, as he went up the hill like a giddy goat, that Time was passing by.

Except for a limp, some bruises and a bump or two, our randy professor got away and lived to tell the tale.

Not everyone got so lucky!

Like the ones who met our second man-eater, albeit a singing one.

'Whenever I sing why do you step out into the balcony?' she asked one of her lovers.

'To make sure the neighbours don't think I'm doing you forcibly!' said he.

But we are getting ahead of the story here. From one of the cottages, you will hear the delightful dulcet tones of an early morning classical *raga* rise clear into the thin air. Its our Lady off Babylon.

'Having swallowed a hundred mice, the cat goes off on a pilgrimage!' her cook gossips.

He has known her for years and if you have the time, he will tell you of one who has once tracked, poached, hunted, ambushed, snared and trapped men with impunity like Salome of the Seven Veils. A perfect man-snare! You could say she was a control freak in some ways. With little control on her arrival on to the stage of life, she was determined to boss over all those who came into her orbit. But life is so iffy, so random, only fools believe they are in control.

'She's a Peeping Tom who loves looking through the keyhole, always wanting a preview—even when she could walk in at the door!' Other folks tell me.

There was a time, in her distant youth, when she was a beautiful woman. She was tall with a handsome face and twinkling almond-shaped eyes, and pendulous breasts, like over-ripe mangoes that threatened to spill out of her clothes.

Apparently, her youth was a talent hunt for the ideal idiot or a marionette whose strings she'd control. I believe, it was all a perfectly pleasant affair while it lasted.

Predictably no one made the grade!

On one such occasion, her two-timing led to a Bollywood filmy-style finish. On one side stood a scrawny brigadier, a long-suffering widower and on the other side a police officer on his third re-treading. The twain had been recipients of her affections in different towns in the plains.

As Lady Luck would have it, the duo found themselves in the hills, arriving at Blueburn Cottage together, almost falling over each other. Their paths merged on this quiet hillside. Two gladiators confronted each other: an aging lion sizing up a spent tiger, trying to beard our man-eater in her own den.

Sparks flew. A frisson of excitement raced through her heart. It was time for a final resolution. At the decisive moment, the reluctance had melted from her voice, replaced in its stead by a note of resentment.

'Life gives you two when you can't take even one!' she moaned.

With the naiveté of a child, she extricated herself from a messy situation by breaking out into song. In the strained circumstances, all she could manage was a weak thin thing with no soul in it, a ghost of a melody. It had the familiar hum that shipwrecked sailors had heard in the Land of the Lotus Eaters.

Ask for her now and you'll find one who's been too long in a hot bath—so coarsened out of all likeness to the bright young thing, who in her youth, had taken Lucknow University by storm.

No longer does she venture out during the day, but only at night, with the stars for company. Wearing a veil, she stirs, stealthily like a ghost and flits around the hills humming the same tune without the words.

There are no second chances in the man-eating business except when our man-eaters end up as trophies on their own walls. This happened to Meeta, quite a heart breaker, and a man-muncher herself. Enveloped in her chiffons and georgettes, she possessed an hourglass figure and a great dress sense, always revealing more than she concealed. Married to a man much older than herself, whom she'd leave in the care of the household help in Mumbai, she trawled the station's aging bachelors during the summer months.

I was there when she attached herself to Mr Limp, the withering scion of one of our old families who had a lineage longer than his arm. But the word was out—his brains were addled, as useless as a brush without bristles. One evening, he invited us for dinner.

'What's special?' I asked.

'Get a taste of it fresh, straight off the pan! Meet my new conquest!' Limp bragged.

When we arrived at their cottage, inexplicably Meeta was sulking. She had a pout all through the evening until the old man stepped out of his bedroom with an exquisite enamelled necklace in his quivering hands. A smile, broad as a mile, lit up her face. She felt the inlay with a caressing movement. Her fingers touched and felt the delicate green and red. If you looked carefully, both the smile and the movement revealed Meeta. She loved beautiful things, but, above all, jewels. It was her single deepest passion. There was not a stone she would leave unturned or nothing she would not do to get hold of anyone's heirlooms.

She sailed through life taking, only taking, and never giving. And if you looked carefully, you'd notice she had a unique gift for converting people to her sins. It was a religious belief with her. She measured the world with one yardstick—her own—judging people solely by their position, flattering the rich while ignoring the poor and the humble.

'The closest she got to education was that she was born in a little shack outside the gates of St George's College!' whispered Mrs Gupp, in my ear.

That's how things were rolling till her wimpish son met this Hi-Tech girl from the plains—her hair was short, her skirt shorter and she short-circuited what little was left of the boy's muddled brains.

Though I must say, all of us smiled as we wished the young couple well, and things were going that way, or at least till the time it occurred to Meeta that the young bride's jewellery trousseau was unsafe in the set of rooms in the hotel.

It was this very edifice that Mr Limp wrapped up in the throes of love, had earlier painstakingly built. Right up to the 1960s, one would see him drive past, on to the road to Park Estate, in an old Willy's Jeep with a trailer in tow, full of the usual accoutrements of construction—gravel, cement, lime, wooden beams, rafters, door-frames, paint drums, basins and WCs too!

'Sala! Ek Taj Mahal Agra mein, Aur ek yahan!' (Damn! One Taj Mahal in Agra and *now* one here!), the bazaar *gupp* went.

But we've digressed. Let me take you back to the tale of the vulnerable trousseau. Meeta took her spanking new daughter-in-law, Miss Hi-Tech to the local bank, to her locker.

'I'll talk to the Bank Manager,' she explained. 'We can operate it jointly.'

That done, everything else went well. The hotel was full. The family jewels were stashed away in the vault—safe and sound.

Awaking rather late one day, she found Hi-Tech's door shut.

'Must be nursing a hangover,' she reassured herself.

As the hours ticked by, concern rose and the door was forced open. The room was empty.

'Ah! She must have gone for a walk,' she explained to the room-bearers.

She was right. Miss Hi-Tech *had* indeed gone for a walk—a very long walk. She'd run away!

Later, much later, they found that the bank locker had been picked clean!

'Easy come! Easier go!' nodded the wags.

Whatever happened to Miss Hi-Tech? You wonder. When last heard of, she had gone back to Delhi, moved in with her ex-boss, and sued Meeta and her son for torture, harassment and making unreasonable demands under the provisions of the Anti- Dowry Act!

Then there is our other man-eater, a certain Miss Tuffet, whom we too shall call *chutail*. What does that mean? Don't fret! Even I thought it was a weird name until I learnt from my friends that it was a loosely applied term by the residents of the nearby villages to describe a lady who has been set free, or on the loose or simply unattached and available.

And the more homes she's walked out of, or so I'm told, increases the value of the *chutail*. After all, one must pay more for extra expertise.

Initially, I was convinced it was just another sexist word in the lexicon of a male-dominated society. I saw no reason to change my opinion when I met this rosy-cheeked girl fresh out of school. Barely sixteen, she had eloped with a young entrepreneur—a picture-perfect couple, winners of a made-for-each-other contest. It was too good to last for aren't the first blooms of spring usually battered by a passing hailstorm?

A messy divorce ensued. It made no difference for she did not wait to catch her breath, as it were, and was on the prowl again. She was looking for her perfect mate, partner and lover and friend. Of course there's no such thing that exists. Man is a bundle of imperfections. Only weeks afterwards, she'd moved in with a scruffy freak of unknown vintage. The arrangement, I guess if you could call it that, worked well for two years until things soured; he threw her out, sold the house and was last heard of babbling in the smoking dens of Saharanpur.

Surely that was the end of her! We could not have got it more wrong. Nothing could put her down. She bounced back into the social circuit and hey presto—she had snagged a rich babbler minus brains. But Miss Tuffet was not looking for brains. She had already proved that she had enough grey matter by moving in with her hands in *his* pockets. That was her preferred position. Happy to report that as I write, they are living in these hills happily ever after.

'That's only till she's eaten him up and spat him out too!' predicts Mrs Gupp.

Chapter 4

Schools For Scandal

Abhagele khane belama jahile pani andhiberi

NEWARI PROVERB

(There's always a storm when the unlucky sit down to dine.)

'How delicious is this coldness in the Hills! It is just as wet, windy and wretched as in England!' exclaimed Fanny Parkes. Was it just that? Or is there something in the air here that makes it a perfect place for love, passion and seductions? In spring, the sap begins to rise, the hillside resonates with tales of lust.

It's way beyond 'coveting your neighbour's house, his wife, his man-servant, his maid-servant, his ox, his ass, anything that is your neighbours'.

These hills have never had any official purpose. Arrived here, the visitor feels a heady rush of freedom, a sense of suddenly breaking loose from constraints which often leads to aberrations. Mostly, the locals tend to do their own thing, leaving you alone until you step on someone's toes.

In the days of the Raj, this was where folks let their hair down and were not averse to a little romance or wenching. An able ally was the stationmaster who, whenever the young men debouched at the railway station, would direct them to lonely grass widows teaching in our schools. Many of these boys were from lonely outposts, thirsting for companionship. Only he knew whether Jill had come up the hill or not, and knew too whether it was politic or not to send Jack up for company. For years he moved the pawns much to his amusement. Then one day, a particularly dashing gallant sought his guidance. The prospects sounded topping, so up he came and had all he wanted and much more. Within four days the stationmaster received the laconic message: 'Send second relief!'

At other times, an absent husband would turn up without warning, play spoil sport and find himself at the wrong corner of the eternal triangle. Predictably, all hell would break loose. In order to avoid such unfortunate mix-ups, some of the boarding houses introduced a separation-bell, which was rung at four in the morning to warn adulterers to get back to their rooms before they were discovered by irate husbands or wives. A naughty place this was in the good old days! And believe me such entertainment still exists on our quiet hillsides.

Take, Mr Jerk, a grammarian who recently rushed to the civil hospital in an awful state in the 108 ambulance with cuts and bruises to his face and a suspected broken shin.

'What happened?' asked the doctor. Was this a medico-legal case?

'It's my wife; she had one of her nightmares.'

'You must be joking! How could she do this while she was asleep?'

'Oh! No doctor, it was only when she shouted in her sleep, "Quick, go, my husband's coming home," that, without a moments delay, I jumped out of the first-floor window.'

Our schools, which despite all their moral science classes (or is it because of them?), have their fair share of scandals involving rakes, vamps, grass widows, bored housewives and school principals. An anonymous doggerel printed in the *Civil and Military Gazette* holds a mirror to the town:

I had a little husband
Who gave me all his pay
I left him for Mussoorie
A hundred miles away,
I dragged my little husband's name
Through heaps of social mire,
And joined him in November
As good as you'd desire.

After all how can we with all our roses be without thorns? On the surface, our residential schools, modelled on the English public schools, are paragons of virtue. Our students wear blazers, play cricket on the pitch and help in governance by sharing the prefect system. But the insular atmosphere remains a twin-edged sword—it protects the school's denizens from the depredations of the outside world, but promises no protection from hazards lurking within the schools' gates.

Progress has come to our charitable trusts. In one, a great indoor gymnasium has been built; seating capacity of over a thousand, sliding seats—you name it, they've got it. Only trouble is that none of the students go anywhere near it—they prefer fiddling around with their play-stations, and iPod nanos.

But the men who saw tomorrow built a new marble-tiled swimming pool with all the accoutrements of a five star hotel. 'If you take a dip,' Mr Builder Bear, the proud contractor told me as he rubbed his hand in glee: 'You have the illusion of being in an infinity pool.'

I'm told its waters are clean and it's not on account of its filtration plant—no one ventures near the pool. Unless you include the monkeys from the adjoining forest, dropping by for a dip. Lucky monkeys!

'Food, what can I say about that?' wonders Peggy Hodgson who was in one of our boarding schools, from 1947 to 1954. She writes: 'Pish-pash—one of the best dishes on the menu. Well! You either loved it or hated it. It began with variations of dal, rice and meat cooked together—looked horrible, like something to feed to the dog. Rice and meat was over-boiled in it but it was flavoursome with cinnamon and cardamoms and maybe some other spices. I'm not a gourmet, just a glutton.'

'Another dish, short-lived but memorable, was sausages. There must have been potatoes and vegetables with it but all we looked forward to was Friday nights for the two, or was it three black sausages, about the size of two flanges of a man's middle finger or mine. One could say it looked like what the dog left behind—delicious!'

'The only other bit of lunches and dinners I remember was spinach, for if we asked Snowball what we were getting, he would reply 'grass' when it was vegetable. We had boiled eggs on Sundays for two years and then they disappeared as did the tea-cakes. Otherwise breakfasts were the same through every year: dal one day, *dalia* (porridge) the next spread thinly over a dinner plate. I'd eat the former and give away the latter. Once, they must have been running short of dal and mixed it with pumpkin; no, that's a lie—pumpkin pudding is great! Anyway, I ate the mixture and heaved it up ten minutes later! Luckily, we also got three slices of brown bread, one dry, one with a scrape of some thin jam and the last with a scrape of white grease.

A mug of tea, which I tasted every first day then left alone for the rest of the school year for there were always glasses of water at each meal. Tea was tea and the same three slices of bread. So, for two meals I had bread and water!'

But no bread and butter for Mr Glutton, a housemaster in one of our institutions—a confirmed 'foodie'—the monotonous school diet of pumpkin cooked in meat and rice was not for him. At home, his dining table groaned under the load of victuals brought as gifts by the boys under his charge—guava cheese, rhododendron squash, cucumber relish and blackberry jam.

'Chopsi!' You would hear him say. 'Bring me that mango pickle from Hyderabad on your return from the summer break.'

'And Baljit! What's wrong with you? Cat got your tongue or what? Where is my game pickle?'

One day Baljit had simply had it. Enough was enough. For ten years in school, at the end of each term break, he had brought the old codger quail, wild-boar or partridge pickle. So, this time, just before the end of the winter vacations, he shot two crows, pickled them in the usual condiments and stuffed them into a glass jar and presented them to the housemaster.

The term passed off peacefully. Baljit was pleased as punch at having finally cooked the old man's goose.

At the end of term, he couldn't resist taking a last pot-shot, to sort of rub it in by asking the housemaster:

'Sir! Shall I bring you some more quail pickle?'

'Yes! Please do!' nodded Glutton, and as almost an afterthought added: 'But do me a favour, please could you bring the feathers along too?'

Within the hallowed precincts of the schools all may seem calm, sort of under control with not a ripple, until one shakes it a bit and the bubbles of dormant desires blink on the surface.

My friend, Patrick Corbett, who was a student here in the 1940s, tells me that on one occasion, the wise, grey-heads of a school conducted interviews for teachers. In their combined wisdom, they selected the best from a bevy of bright busy bodies.

Having arrived in the insular world of the school, one of the new appointees, a stout matron struck up what seemed like a very close friendship with one of the younger lady teachers. Soon the two were almost inseparable.

'Wonderful! Those two are *so* close!' proclaimed Mr Know It All, the wise old Chairman of the school, telling the others, 'Good for the morale of the others!'

To encourage camaraderie, they were even allotted a set of rooms' right next to each other on the first floor of the girl's dormitory.

'It keeps discord at bay!' said the principal parroting Mr Know It All. Yes! It certainly appeared good for the morale of the others too!

Things worked perfectly well or you could say maybe just a bit *too* well! One windswept night, the lights blinked as the matron, the one with the rasping voice, made her way to the toilets at the end of the veranda (for that's where they had those old thunder-boxes). Groping in the dark, she missed a step, lurched clean over the railings and plunged head first into the ravine down below.

The sonic boom of her scream shattered the sound barrier, rattling the windowpanes of the boy's hostel, arousing them from their dreams.

They took off down the corridors, lunged into the soporific darkness of the yawning cliff to discover a dishevelled figure, lying spreadeagled on one of the bramble bushes that covered the hillsides. Under the glare of torchlight they turned her over. She looked like a fright! Now, it was their turn to be surprised.

Our matron turned out to be no 'she'. The unflattering torch lit up the anatomy of a perfect male of the species.

Our 'she' had all this time really been a 'he'!

Now that was definitely good for the morale.

Old timers believe one of our schools has come up on an old burial site, with djinns or ghosts hovering around. Or how else can one explain the troubles that constantly seem to plague them?

For instance, the Contortionist, the principal whose wife had left him for reasons unknown, was going through a bad patch. Late in the evenings you could say, he would find his legs involuntarily carrying him to one of the lady teacher's cottage.

As luck would have it, at the time, the school management was enmeshed in a sticky labour dispute with the kitchen staff. Things were not going too well when on that fateful day he slunk off for a tryst.

Scrawny, unkempt, unshaven and pissed off, the workers gathered in the middle of the night for a Che Guevara-type raid. With alarming alacrity, they surrounded the oak fringed home, thudding on the door with angry fists. No response. They knocked again. No response. The fat cook, a tub of lard, pushing the others aside, lunged at the door. The bolt snapped. The crowd poured in.

The Contortionist was nowhere to be seen. Had he done the Indian rope trick or vanished up the chimney? Yes! They looked for him! From bedroom to bathroom, from under the kitchen sink to the veranda, even the store was not left out. But of the venerable man there was no trace!

As they were about to leave, one busy body, a complete spoilsport, turned around, came back into the teacher's bedroom and for some inexplicable reason, fiddled with the handle of an old metal cupboard.

The door clanged open to reveal him all twisted up like an accomplished yogi inside!

Was it panic or guilt or a touch of both?

It wasn't as if the two lovers had been caught *in flagrante delicto*! Either way, the game was up. The humiliation complete. For that very same day had he not waxed eloquent at the morning assembly on the evils of adultery?

My friend, author Bill Aitken still feels: 'Ah! What a great advertisement for steel almirahs!'

I wouldn't argue with that.

Few could expect the mother of all pranks in a staid school, that created more tremors than the great earthquake of 1905. In this tale, just for our purposes, our hero is Brother Always, sworn to celibacy, nevertheless, given to flaunting a soft spot for one of the pretty teachers. If only he'd left it at that, there would have been no tales to tell. Given his rub-ins with the senior boys, who too nursed a secret crush on the same lady, things only went from bad to worse, worse to vicious. It was time for action. A plan was put in place, as one of the day-scholars was nominated to have a wedding card printed. There were no shortcuts. The card was composed, proof-read and printed. In gold-embossed letters, it announced the forthcoming wedding of Brother Always and Miss Blinkers on such and such day.

These were dutifully mailed to every personage in town—the District Administration, the Board of Directors, the Bar Council, the Hotelier's Association, the Trader's Guild, the Rotary Club, the Press Club, and the Parent-Teacher Association and to everyone who was someone. If you didn't get one, you obviously had not made it in life. The ensuing fireworks lit up the hills right down to the valley floor.

'It's rumblings would have done any volcano proud!' reminisces one of the old retired teachers.

Result? Curtains for Brother Always. Sequestered, he was sent off to do a year's penance in an isolated monastery in the backwaters of Allepey. Our pretty teacher was given till the end of the school term to sort out her personal life. That proved to be quite easy. Immediately, she attached herself to the Maths master.

When reports last came in, the school was stuck trying to solve that theorem!

In the 1960s, the hills were the favourite destination of missionaries recuperating from the rigours of life in the plains. In 1888, Flora Annie Steel's advice was: 'The annual vacation to the hills should also be regularly taken; not because we are ill, but to keep off disease, it rarely cures it, and then the only alternative is to give up work and go to England. If advice given above is followed, life may be spent usefully and happily in this country for years.'

Another complained: 'I really did imagine I might venture to walk a few miles on a cloudy day in June, and the effect was very alarming. As I lay on my couch feeling as if insects were traversing my brain, and an iron band tightened round my brows, I perceived how dearly we may have to pay for imitating the apostolic mode of walking about exposed to the sun.'

Other schools specialized in educating missionary children and letting them loose on the world.

In the 1960s, one school laid such stress upon good moral values, that if you dared light a single incense stick, you were labelled a devil worshipper!

After a series of unfortunate mishaps involving the faculty in which one inexplicably fell off the balcony, another sleep walked, others started seeing apparitions and a few began speaking in tongues, that a ghost-buster was urgently summoned from overseas to exorcise the spirits. Unfortunately, that did not work either as he too began babbling like an idiot before falling down a precipice.

While the school was preoccupied with these troubles, the real devil (one of those comely flower children from the 1970s), an old alumni no doubt, crept in through the chaos quietly one day in search of work. She slipped through the administrative sieves to plonk herself in their midst. Her outstanding contribution revealed itself six months later. It was found that she was making far *too* many 'promotional trips' every weekend to the metros accompanied by the balding headmaster.

'Catching up with old alumni,' or 'raising funds for the school,' they'd chirp to explain away their jaunts.

Sadly, the nitpicking auditors began objecting to travel vouchers billing the school for only a *single*-room on their every absence from the school. The cat was out of the bag! The news raced around the hillside like a raging forest fire. As usual, the school administration was the last to find out what every little kid in school already knew.

As I write, the school has no principal or PRO.

New applicants please note that while the salary is nothing much to write home about, the fun and games are thrown in for free.

In another august institution, one morning, Mr WW Hayes, a not-so-bright variety of teacher, braced himself for prayers in the morning assembly. With gusto, eyes shut, he belted out the hymn 'Onward Christian soldiers! Onward off to war!' and onward off the stage he fell onto the floor down below!

A hush descended upon the assembly. Silence reigned!

'Come on! What's wrong with you?' he yelled as he limped back on stage: 'Raise your spirits!' Afterwards hobbling out of the hall, he was heard to mumble: 'Yes! Raise your spirits. Unfortunately at my age, that's about all that rises!' Unknowingly, he won the thrifty sobriquet—Wobbly Wobbly Hayes.

'It's all about thrift Sa'ab!' says Dayal Singh, a bearer in one of the private hostels owned by some of our leading lights.

'After breakfast, the bearers would drain the last dregs of milk from every cup, through a sieve into a jug,' he tells me shrugging his shoulders. 'It sufficed for making tea in the evening for the whole hostel.'

No wonder then, the school's motto proudly proclaimed: 'Waste not, want not!'

Later day entrants in the school business were of the get-rich-quick variety and turned up in the 1960s. Most perished on the wrong side of the starting line. One sprouted near the town's park, and was infamous for bullying, where three boys went down the hillside and only two came back. What happened to the third? He was found trussed up two days later in a hessian bag murdered by his friends.

Another, which luckily for all of us, has long since folded up, moved from one rented property to the other until both funds and pupils were exhausted. It was called the 'Remainder Theorem School', fuelled as it was by the dropouts, leftovers, dregs, rejects and recycled ones from the other schools and its illustrious school history was a list of scuffles, stabbings and knifings. It would have put any penitentiary to shame. The day-scholars were very popular for all the wrong reasons: they smuggled in vodka concealed in water bottles and mobiles wrapped in foil, cleverly placed between sandwiches in their tiffin boxes.

Kala School is named after the black habits of the nuns of Waverley Convent located on a hill once owned by the Begum Samru of Sardhana. There's a lot of monkeying around and it's not just the troupes that roam the grounds raiding the day-scholar's lunch boxes, textbooks, and satchels. Sometimes, the students too fool around by trying to run away. Are they homesick or school sick? No one will tell. But if you spot a cloister of nuns gathered at Town Square, peering into cars streaming past, be assured they are not cadging a lift. They are looking for runaways.

Running away from it all was not a solution for some. I find a record in another school's register of a master and his wife—a perfect example of what awful results can mature from petty considerations. Mrs Fennimore, the wife of a schoolmaster was inextricably enmeshed in a puerile defamation lawsuit, which was extremely distasteful to Mr Fennimore. The fat was in

the fire as the whole affair drove him to a terrible solution. On 24 November, 1917, finding his wife lying on her side in sound sleep, he shot her through the back of the head. For no accountable reason, he slipped the revolver under her pillow, calmly moved to the lavatory, three rooms away from the bedroom, leaned on his loaded rifle and shot himself too!

Again, in the same institution, another headmaster's wife fired at a junior mistress, wounding her. She was arrested for an attempt to murder. The school records are silent on the motive and the case is lost in the grey areas of crime detection.

The Arya Kanya Pathshala, one of the vernacular schools started in 1910 at Kirkland Estate, is today a girl's college. It has had colourful people at the helm of affairs including the old vixen Mrs Hathisingh, who also bred dogs, but hers were of dubious origin. She once fought a ten-year case against a woman from Calcutta who had sued her for selling her a golden Cocker Spaniel, which after a few weeks turned completely black!

'She was most unattractive, and the ugliest woman you could possibly imagine. One still can't figure out why men were so attracted to her. Was it because she was dominating? There was RKV, the Municipal Chairman, only too willing to do her bidding, and old Colonel Powell used to call her Neela Rani or the Blue Queen!', a friend of mine, who knew her, told me.

When she died, a man from Saharanpur turned up and paid for the funeral and simply vanished forever. Then there was Bandhu, the Station House Officer of police; he too was a regular pilgrim to her place.

Was it sex appeal or was she just a petty manipulator who would get men to do her odd favours? No one knows.

My father's relations with Mrs Hathisingh can at best be described as bitter. I think she found the act of having the electric meter read or paying her bills offensive? Was it against her religion? Or had single-blessedness soured her to life's feast?

Who knows?

The devil's advocate whispers in my ears: 'Did she nurse a secret crush for the tall, dark, handsome youth who'd turn up at her gate, notepad in hand and *all* the fellow was really interested in was reading her electric meter!' And I see no reason not to believe these voices.

As he touched the latch on the gate, all hell broke loose—yapping Pekinese, confused Cocker Spaniels and snapping Daschounds would be snapping at him. Out on a limb, distressed at one unread meter, my father complained to RKV. He threw the book at her for obstructing a government servant on duty. Mrs Hathisingh was to nurse a permanent grudge against meter-readers to the end of her days.

I met her in the winter of her life, on my way to school in the 1960s; I heard a gruff voice growl: 'Oye *laundey*! (urchin), What's your name?'

'Ganesh, ma'am,' startled I mumbled. 'Saili!' I added. You could have cut the early morning chill with a knife.

'Are you that Mukand Ram Saili's son?' my inquisitor grunted. 'Yes! Ma'am,' the words spilled out of me.

'Is he not dead yet?'

'No!' I assured her. 'He's fine.' That said, I took off down the hill.

She had definitely not forgotten my father!

Over the wall from the girls' school, was the boys' school whose legendary principal, Amrit Sagar Malhotra came from Abottabad after partition. Modelling himself on the old grammarian, he ran a tight ship, until one morning, a cloud crept over his face when he saw there were not enough students in the afternoon assembly! A storm was brewing.

With Chandan Singh, the loyal school peon in tow, he stomped off to the local cinema hall.

One of those old truants remembers the shivers it sent down their spines as they heard his voice boom over the sound track: 'Gates shut! Lights on!'

The projectionist froze. The picture stopped. The lights came on.

Out of the cinema-hall's darkened innards poured a steady stream of blinking errants who walked straight into the principal. Ashen-faced, they were lined up and marched in deafening silence back to school.

'Fall into two rows facing each other!' snapped Mr Malhotra, as he proceeded to rap them on their knuckles. But his hands were tired soon and so he told them: 'And now slap each other hard, two times!'

Ah! Those sepia-toned days of nostalgia, 'Spare the rod, and spoil the child!' he said.

Spoilt, believe me, no one gets at our Babel College housed in the Cereal House built in 1870. And who was Cereal? He was a Canadian

missionary, an amateur photographer, who met his end as he cycled off the road into a gaping defile near the church. The school offers excellent courses in Urdu, Punjabi, Hindi and Hindustani to research scholars, wanderers and lost souls.

'The school is the visa-section of the American Embassy. Green Card guaranteed!' a grump tells me. The allusion is to some of their teacher's multitasking skills—deftly they move from interactive walks teaching Hindi, classroom to bedroom, before brushes with the *Kama Sutra* and marriages with *firangi* students to relocate abroad on a new-found spouse's visa.

No visas were needed in another of our schools as it set a record in 1949. It was a year that shall be remembered when just about every boy doing senior Cambridge failed!

And in the same year someone stole the Master's dinner from the mess servants, leaving the poor man hungry and inconsolable. The next morning was the month-end visit to town.

The master-on-duty addressed the boys: 'Someone stole the Master's dinner last night. If the thief steps forward he will be on detention, if he doesn't step forward the entire school will be punished for the crime of one boy! Remember too that you shall not bear false witness against your neighbour!'

No one owned up.

'Right boys, I will count to three. If the thief steps forward, he will be punished, if he doesn't, your visit to town is cancelled!'

Sure enough, at the count of three, a boy stepped forward. He was detained; the rest of the school went to town. At the end of term, teachers would escort their students' home.

As the train station arrived, the boy who had confessed to stealing the dinner said: 'Thank you sir for being such a brilliant teacher,' adding as an afterthought, '... and by the way sir I did not steal the teacher's food!'

'Then what made you confess?'

'Sir I knew the real culprit. But, he did not have the courage to confess. It would have been unfair for the entire school to suffer just because of the cowardice of that one boy.'

On school opening day, if you go past the gates of our boarding schools, you shall see their entrances choked with moping parents arriving to drop off their children.

In the 1960s, Saxenaji of Benares had come to drop off his six-year old daughter to school. Like any doting parent, he wanted to be assured that his daughter had settled down comfortably, so he decided to extend his stay at the Connaught Castle hotel by a couple of days. Browsing through a book at the Cambridge Book Depot, he bumped into a person who seemed familiar, yet he could not place him.

'Don't you recognise me? You're from Benares? No? Aren't you? I've seen you so many times at the *paan*-shop in Gadolia.'

'Yes! Yes!' nodded Saxenaji. He knew the face, but he couldn't put a peg on it. Just to be friendly, he asked: 'Oh yes! What are you doing here?'

'I've just joined a local school as a science teacher.'

'Good for you! Come. Let's have a drink in my room,' said Saxenaji, scratching his head and for the life of him, he could not remember the man's name. You couldn't bark: 'What's your name?' mulled Saxenaji. It would be too rude to ask, especially if the man seemed to know you already.

Returning to the hotel, one drink led to another and on to several others. At the end of the bash, Saxenaji noticed that his newfound friend was seven sails in the wind, definitely in no shape to walk four miles back on the unlit road to the school.

Prudently, he tucked his guest into bed and went off to sleep. No problem.

Or so he thought.

Next morning he found his guest still deep asleep. Stirring out of bed, he tried to nudge his Sleeping Beauty awake! He shook him. Not a whisper. His guest did not stir. He couldn't. For he was dead!

Saxenaji stood there stunned like a dying duck in a thunderstorm.

And if you think all hell broke loose after that, you're right. Everything imaginable hit the fan. And all that hit the ceiling was not necessarily evenly distributed—police, post-mortem and publicity. In distant Benares, the local rags picked up the refrain of conspiracy theories. Why would he have invited a man he hardly ever associated with in his own hometown, to his room for drinks? Was it murder or poisoning? Or perhaps a property angle?

Luckily, for him, the post mortem concluded that the man's weak heart had given in.

'Never invite a man you don't know to your hotel room for a drink!' he advised me thirty years later with a shudder, adding: 'Especially if you don't even know his name!'

Chapter 5

The Misfits

Chottoh koh badoh, badoh koh bagh, bagh koh jibalo, jibalo koh aag

GARHWALI PROVERB

(The small loses to the big, the big to the leopard, the leopard to the snare and the snare loses to the forest fire.)

Occasionally, our newlyweds on honeymoon provide a frisson of excitement to the town. Their antics make good copy, grist for the mill as it were, to the forty-odd journalists who have to fill up reams of blank paper as local news that is hard to come by.

Take for instance, a young couple that checked into one of the hotels. Next morning the husband went for a shower, which was alright.

Trouble began when he tried to get out. The door would not budge. Of course it couldn't.

His beautiful bride of last night had locked him and eloped with her college-going lover, who had secretly trailed the couple here. When the hotel staff finally forced opened the door, they found our bridegroom of one night in his underwear. Oh! The unkindest cut of all was that the crazed lovers had taken with them the poor man's luggage—clothes and all!

It is tough chasing someone through the bazaar in your underwear!

In another guesthouse, the cashier had a polite notice hanging behind the front desk. It said: 'Have you left anything?' An irate customer, feeling short-changed told the cashier: 'You should change it to "Have you anything left?"'

And it's usually the honeymooners who have nothing left. A young couple checked into a hostelry, where soon after, the bride again went missing. Awaking bleary eyed from his sleep, the husband went to the front desk to ask if they had seen his wife. The receptionist told the waiters, the waiters told the housemaid, the housemaid told the room service and the room service told the storekeeper. They all shook their heads in disbelief. For the front desk manager had gone missing too.

If you've guessed this one out, you're right! The two had gone arm in arm, over meadow and farm to walk into the sunset.

While we are talking of hotels, most of them, big or small, have one thing in common—sometimes a guest flinches the linen, the cutlery, and at times even an occasional TV. Nandu's (my friend, once owner of the Savoy) favourite story is of how one customer drove off with a mattress rolled up on the carrier. When the manager realised what had happened, he phoned the police at the toll barrier, and the police stopped the car and took possession of the missing mattress. Promptly, the owner of the car blamed the driver for the theft, but the driver responded, 'Sir, you asked me to pick up two mattresses, and now you are blaming me for stealing this one!'

Then, there are those tourists who leave their belongings behind, or if not their belongings, their fellow travellers. The day after a group of jolly, booze-guzzling young men left their room, the housekeeper opened a cupboard to have a dead body tumble out on top of her. In another hotel, a box bed was found stuffed with the corpse of a young lady. Both cases remain unsolved. Trying to match this enterprise were some young men from Panipat who stabbed to death one of their companions and left the body in the cemetery. But they left a trail of clues behind and were caught a few days later.

An old guide from the 1930s has more tales of infidelity:

'A pretty young thing had daily to be left alone for hours while the breadwinner went off to work at his office. Being almost a wise man, he knew the perils of living in a crowded place, but lacking real wisdom, he distrusted his wife and used to lock her up in their one room apartment. He used to slip the key back, just in case she had to get out in an emergency. Returning home, a call at the door would warn the prisoner that it was time to pass the key back so he could let himself in.

The months sped by happily. He was pleased with himself for having found such a perfect solution to the temptations of the flesh and she was glad to have found a perfect solution to get a taste of the forbidden. While the husband was away, her lover crept into her room and left well before the husband came home.

And so it merrily carried on, except for holidays. The lover boy came with mechanical regularity till Nemesis arrived disguised as an ordinary tummy upset. Try as hard as he would, the husband could not control the rumblings in his stomach and arrived home early. His urgent knocking for the key was unanswered at first.

Then the key tinkled out. The moment of his entry was the moment of forgetting even why he had come home. In a single sweep he saw the base of the eternal triangle before he set his eyes on his cowering wife, for in a single-room there was no space to hide her lover boy.

The two men sized each other in deafening silence and the husband simply managed to utter: "Now you go!"

With incredible control, the husband went back to the office, took a day's leave, and ensured that his wife had packed every little trinket he had ever given, took her to Dehra and bought her a ticket—one way—to her home in the plains. Before the train steamed out he turned his back on her—forever.'

Some good souls built a hospital for the missionaries holidaying here eighty years ago and after a philanthropic restoration, it continues to serve the community's medical needs. Waiting my turn on a bench outside the futuristic pathology lab, I was witness to the following exchange:

'But I can't believe it!' exclaimed a distressed Mr R, 'Pregnant? How can that be? I've always been so bloody careful.'

'Now, now,' clucked the wife comforting him. 'What makes you think it's your fault?'

'We are all idlers here,' wrote a visitor in 1858, 'We are all sick, or supposed to be so; or we have leave on private affairs. Some of us are up here for a month between musters. We are in the good graces of our colonel, and our general—the general of our division, a very old gentleman.

Let us now while away the morning. Let us call on some of the grass widows. There are lots of them here, civil and military. Let us go first to Mrs Merrydale, the wife of our old friend Charley, of the two hundredth and ten regiment. Poor fellow! He could not get leave, and the doctors said another hot summer in the plains would be the death of his wife.

By the October, the season is over and everybody here is on the move—going down the hill as it was called.'

He sums up the events of that season thus: 'Four young men were victimised; two at cards and two at billiards. Two duels were fought on the day after the ball. In one of these duels an officer fell dead. In another the offending party grievously wounded his antagonist. There were two elopements. Mrs Merrydale went off with Lieutenant Maxwell, leaving her children under the care of the servants, until her husband came to take them away. Mrs Hastings, who used to bore us about the duties of a wife, carried off that silly boy Stammersleigh.'

Life in the hills was centred on clubs like the Happy Valley Club which folded soon after the Second War, so our club going gentry founded the Rotary Club in 1947. I have it on the authority of our locals, that those applicants the Masonic Lodge delays, join the Rotary Club, those the Rotary fobs join the Lions Club, and those the Lions won't have split alike the atom and from the fission are reborn a plethora of more Lions Club. Often you will find banners proclaiming the new *Loins* Club Hills Chapter.

In the 1970s, my friend, author Ruskin Bond had the dubious distinction of becoming the founder President of the first Lions' Club. After the second meeting, he fled when he found his new friends starting to call him *Loin* Bond!

Dr G, a dedicated Rotarian of forty years standing, narrates one of his favourite joke of a small boy, who asks his mother: 'Mama how do lions make love?'

'I don't know,' she says. 'All your father's friends are Rotarians!'

And keeping an eagle eye on your perfect vision are the opticians. They ensure everyone in the resort keeps a sharp eye on everyone else. The late Mr Short-sighted, the amiable owner of one such establishment had a permanent toilet-brush salesman's smile.

Soon as an old lady walked into the shop, he would whip out an expensive pair of frames, wait for her to put them on, step back like a judge in a beauty contest, with his own spectacles resting on the tip of his nose, flash that million-dollar smile (recently polished by the town's dentist, no doubt!) and exclaim: 'You are looking like queen!' *(sic)*

With the deal concluded, the customer out of earshot, he would throw his head back, give me a knowing wink and cluck: 'Queen? My foot! Ugly old cow! She'll believe anything you say! What lies this wretched stomach makes you tell Saili Sa'ab!'

With the passage of time, as he grew older, the competition from his fellow opticians began to sour him a little. If you so much as dared mention the name of any other person who crafted prescription glasses, he would work himself into a fit: 'You'll go cross-eyed if you buy his wares... That bugger grinds his lenses from soda bottle bottoms!'

Though soda was the last thing on the immaculately turned out Mr Strutter's mind. He was a remnant of the last days of the landed gentry,

'Looking like Queen'

who ran a non-descript store hiring out furniture in town. Think of him, and you see an old aristocrat attired in finery, a rakish silk cap tilting on his head, and a handsome silver-knobbed walking stick, an heirloom no doubt, handed down by his illustrious ancestors.

A genial widower in his sixties, who, from his bungalow on the crest of a hill had seen this place shrug off the air of a fading British resort. He was witness to businessmen from the plains, full of gumption, arrive in large numbers and sweep away the last few British cobwebs.

Trouble came when in his sixties, he aggressively turned transgender—homosexual, heterosexual, pansexual and poly-sexual, from sunrise to dusk stalking the alleys for a pick-up, abandoning all pretence of being a family man. You could say he was gay and happy—all day long. Unfortunately, this accosting of all and sundry, led to rub-ins with the law.

Soon after, he had gained a sufficient measure of infamy. The college boys would tease him about his sexual prowess. Puffing his chest like a pouter pigeon, he would witheringly dismiss them, saying: 'Ever tried a diet of milk and raw eggs?'

Yes! Soda was definitely not on his mind!

One day, as a public member on a house tax committee of the local board, I found myself on the wrong side of the table when Mr Strutter arrived to protest the increase in taxes of his squatter-infested ancestral properties.

'You're being most unfair to me,' he said to us. 'My tenants are not tenants, they are only occupants, who pay no rents and now you too want to raise my house tax!'

I introduced myself. The years peeled away to a time when as a little boy I was in kindergarten with his cute daughters. He looked me up. He looked me down. Rearing himself to his full six-foot hulk, he simply said: '*Barkhurdar! Aana Kabhi theekh sey milaingey!*' (Gentleman! Come over. We must meet properly someday!)

It was my turn to run! As fast as my legs would carry me!

Chapter 6

Mishmash

Hatti cale bajar, Kukur bhuke hajar
NEPALI PROVERB

(When an elephant goes to the market, thousands of dogs bark at it.)

Over the years, these hills have been home to movie actors past and present, beginning in the 1950s with actor Prem Nath and his wife, and the stunningly beautiful Bina Roy who bought a cottage on the lip of Oak Road, facing the Doon valley.

The 1960s saw the handsome Dev Anand and his sultry wife, actress Kalpana Kartik, take over Sisters Cottage opposite Prakash's Store in Sister's Bazaar to put their children into a school. Thespian Victor Banerjee, known for his acting prowess in films like *Shatranj Kay Khiladi*, *Home in the World*, and *A Passage to India* arrived in the 1980s for a film shoot, fell in love with the place and settled in a quiet corner. Tom Alter, grew up in a family of missionaries, went to school here, and his foray into Bollywood began in the 1970s.

As I write, film director Vishal Bhardwaj has just found himself a getaway.

However, there is no getaway for these good folks when they really need a break from their busy lives in the film world. Our schools, clubs and academies will not let them be. Invariably they find themselves being dragged off to be chief guests at all sorts of functions: Founder's day, debates, inter-house matches, fancy fairs, *melas,* fetes, one-act plays and a host of other activities which are of interest only to these institutions.

Knowing how painfully tedious it can be to sit through one of these performances, our celebrities usually try to wriggle out of them by politely declining or saying they are otherwise occupied. On occasions like these, faced with the prospect of having to launch another star hunt, the grumpy school administrators have reportedly been heard to say some very rude things:

'That chap! His contract is longer than his script!'

Or 'You know why folks come to his movies dressed in pyjamas?' 'Because they all know they'll fall asleep anyway.'

'Oh! Forget them all!' shouts the irate headmaster, 'Get someone from the National Academy! They'll never refuse! Not with their children studying here!'

Not everyone studies though. Like the plump Mrs Chettri who lives just outside town, along the old Cart Mackinnon Road, next to a lonesome poultry farm. She is singularly blessed with nine children.

How did she manage that? She is often asked.

'Simple!' she shrugs, adding: 'At dawn the roosters begin to crow and Mr Chettri awakened from his slumber, can think of nothing better to do!'

'The woman who stuttered ended up with eleven children!' The hill folk will tell you.

Forty years ago, this was a second hand-dealer's paradise. Foreign missions started winding up, departing missionaries took to selling off their belongings in elaborate yard sales. The 'Emperor of all wheeler-dealers' was the long in the tooth, lean and cavernous Munna—or so he was called by his friends. One would often bump into him as he made his way on rounds of the various bungalows.

'Given your talents, you should've been a rich man by now!' I said to him. Munna did not wince. He looked me straight in the eye saying: 'Oh! Belt up Saili sahab! It's the curse of us card players. We've spent our lives in a futile wait for the three aces to turn up in a single hand!'

True that! If he wasn't foraging for junk, he'd be playing high stake rummy, while sunning himself in the last patches of sunshine filtering through the bazaar's narrow lanes.

There were times you'd catch his eyes mist over with memories of the days of wine, women and song, then he'd turn his nose up in the air, snootily dismiss the Johnny-come-to-town-lately as greenhorns, still wet behind the ears, by insisting: 'These cheap skates are no *raeeses* for the only true *raees* (a wealthy man) was Ramaria Seth. I'd go to his house to fluff forty-kilo velvet mattresses surrounded by satin-cushioned chairs, the essence of roses, dried fruits, sweetmeats and dancing girls, gyrating on their heels!'

'We buy junk and sell antiques,' could well have been the legend outside Subodh's second-hand shop, adjacent to Munna's humble shack. Rest assured, he was no *raees* either, for you'd find him struggling up the hill, out-of-breath, panting, trying to keep up with the diddle of old junk dealers.You'd see the lines on his face stretch to bursting, worrying that he'd get left behind and miss out on a big deal. As the others went on ahead like a pack of hungry wolves, to encircle the house, chat up the white sahib while he hung around the gate, nervously rubbing his bottom on the boundary pillars before making the final dash into the house.

It's unfair to say that it was just Munna alone who loved playing a game of cards. Today, it's almost the whole town. There's a hotel, where all the card-lovers of northern India congregate. Arrived here, they shoo the wives away, to do the checking in, filling up the guest registers or showing identity proof et al! The gamblers head straight for the rummy tables. It is our dark secret—we live with a tradition of gambling. Don't ask me why. It's there.

Last Diwali, a fine summer palace on the Camel's Back Road was lost and won several times over before dawn.

A stone's throw away is the old Skating Rink, where in 1967, an Autumn Festival was organised in which students of the local schools and colleges staged plays in the evenings.

Under the marquee, a poignant scene from the Hindi writer Guleri's *Usnay Kaha Tha* was unfolding. It's a tragic tale of a soldier dreaming of home as he lies fatally wounded in the battlefield. Guptaji, our teetotaller librarian had the role of Lehna Singh, the brave soldier, who lay with a parched throat, gasping for air.

'*Paani*! *Paani*!' (Water! Water!), he cries.

His comrade, a role played by the impish Salim John, a clerk in a local bank, shoves the army water-canteen into the librarian's mouth. He chokes, thereby doing a very realistic enactment of the dying gurgle!

The audience applauds.

No one knew that Salim John in a moment of levity had slipped local firewater into the water bottle!

But the stench of the local liquor hooch, attracted the attention of the college principal who suspecting sabotage, grabbed an umbrella and dashed on to the stage looking for the saboteur, much in the manner of a valiant knight charging the windmills. The crowd believed that this too was a part of the play and broke into thundering applause.

The curtain dropped. Salim John and Guptaji had melted into the crowd and were nowhere in sight. What lingered was the stink of hooch—pure white lightning from Yamuna bridge.

During the Raj, the colonialists were spoilt rotten by an army of servants. Though by the time I was born, the empire-builders had packed their bags and left, leaving their properties in the hands of estate agents who appointed *chowkidars* (watchmen). Finding themselves with little or almost no work at hand, built little sheds to house their cows.

For the propagation of the bovine species, a male calf was donated to the town and left loose on the streets. *Dimriji ka saand* (the robust bull), which we all affectionately called Ramu, was donated by Gopal Dutt Dimri, the handsome labour union leader of the 1950s.

As children, we'd see Ramu wandering the streets and could easily spot those in need of his stud services—they'd arrive tinkling a cowbell in front of him. Suddenly, he would perk up from his languor, snout in the air, curl his lips in ardour, and he was ready.

There certainly was a job to be done.

Knowingly, we'd wink at each other and say: 'Ramu's got a phone call.'

Understandably, the practice of donating a bull for the purposes of procreation was dispensed with when an over-zealous bull, taking his job too seriously, got carried away and ended up goring an innocent bystander.

Never having taken their work too seriously as the bulls, are some of our failed merchants. Among them was the venerable Mr AP. He had tried his hand at a hundred failed ventures yet breezed through life with nary a care. You name it and he'd done it—from selling properties to starting restaurants, from running stores to running away with it all despite his weighing a hundred and fifty kilos. He was a larger than life character, built like one of those World Wrestling Federation contestants, who swash-buckled through it all to arrive in his eighties safe and sound. I met him at breakfast, working his way through a serving bowl of porridge, several omelettes and a grilled chicken, washed down with a large shot or two of vodka. No! Not for him only the mandated three score and ten. There were many years more!

'You owe so much money to everyone!' His anxious brother quizzed him one day: 'How on earth do you sleep so soundly?' Without batting an eyelid, he shrugged his shoulders: 'Let my creditors lose their sleep. They need to pray. If I die, they lose all the money I owe them! What do I lose?'

He passed away one day, leaving behind a legacy of *gupp*, gossip, tall tales and a crush of people on the cremation grounds.

'Who are all these people?' A friend asked. 'Never knew he had so many friends!'

'Friends? They are no friends of his!' said a bystander. 'They are all moneylenders!'

Losers (if one could call them that!) of another kind were the town's six movie halls as they downed their shutters for the last time! They guaranteed entertainment even if the film was lousy. Take the Electric Picture Palace—opened in 1912 (the year electricity came to town), which with the passage of time had lost some of its spit and polish. Its glory was part of history as were the lumpy seats. Often, they possessed a life of their own, sliding off with a resounding thud, occupant and all, flooring the audience with laughter! In a squall, under the onslaught of rain and hail, the steady tattoo of the tin roof, drummed out the sound track, taking you back to the era of the silent films. Years later, the basement reincarnated as the Jubilee Cinema. They forgot to fix the leak on Picture Palace's roof. Over many monsoons, the rusty water trickled down, staining half Jubilee Cinema's silver screen a dirty brown. Yes! You could still see the film but half in black and white and half in sepia tone!

Who would have dared thought the same thing about the posh Rialto? Trouble was, on many occasions, the inebriated projectionist would get the reels mixed up, with interesting results—those hulking Vikings, slain in skirmishes just half an hour ago, would be back, arisen from the dead, astride their horses, again ready to do battle and die once more!

No such mix-up occurred when I saw *Mughal-e-Azam* in a once-grand-now-shambles theatre. It was a throwback to the days of the Raj where the town's upper crust sat in plush boxes and in the pit down below, a few feet from the screen, crowded the ordinary folks. Even back then, those old enclosures were already shoddy holes with wrecked seats, a stench of spilt alcohol, cigarette butts and body odour. From one of those crumbling boxes, I had watched Anarkali's dance in the hall of mirrors. But for the foul smell, the dance would have been memorable.

Mirroring the end of an era, was the old Basant Cinema, which briefly reincarnated as La Anjuman, though the change of name made little difference—the seeping of sewage from the surrounding hotels drowned out our last cinema hall. Though not before Bir Singh, the agile linesman of the electricity board, accompanied by his sidekick arrived; one must say a little high, for the matinee show at a theatre.

As luck would have it, the 'House Full' sign had just gone up on the barred gates. The booking window had slid shut.

'Two tickets!' the duo yelled at Hector Singh, the hassled Manager. 'Can't you read that board?' said Hector Singh.

'Can't you slip in two folding chairs?' countered the duo.

'Of course I can't!' explained an exasperated Hector. 'It's against the rules!'

'*Arrey!* Bir Singh! Go up that electric pole. Pull out the fuse!' affronted, the sidekick said.

'We're not to be trifled with. Are we?' Bir Singh said.

And that is exactly what they did. Loud whistling catcalls and commotion heralded the extinguishing of light. Pandemonium reigned as the hall plunged into darkness. Pleased with their handiwork our recharged duo strutted off to a nearby teashop.

'*Paise wapis! Paise wapis!*' (Return our money!), yelled the crowd.

The writing on the wall was clear and they could read it. Hector Singh capitulated. The teashop owner lent two folding chairs.

A placated Bir Singh ascended the pole and restored the fuse to its rightful place. The lights blazed once again and our deadly duo lived to tell the tale.

'Even an ant can humble an elephant!' mumbled his sidekick.

'Elephant? Oh! Shut up!' said Bir Singh. 'There are no elephants in this picture!' as he went off to sleep to work off the alcohol.

Not all have lost out in these hills for they have been benevolent to many. Out of the many rags to riches stories, my favourite is of a man who sold the only *lohi* (shawl) he possessed on arrival at the station for twelve annas, set up a teashop and went on to own considerable property here.

Of course, to assure his relatives and associates that he was no rajah, his mode of living remained unchanged from that of the less fortunate past.

Others found ingenuous ways of disclaiming nobility; a redcoat Tommy adopted one of the simplest. He was headed for an amusement centre, the Hakman's Palladium, in heavy rain and that necessitated a rickshaw ride.

'Well,' said the spiffy lad at his destination, '*Kitna* paisa?' to which the rickshaw pullers replied most reasonably: '*Bara* anna' (Remember, in those days, 16 annas made up one rupee).

'Garn!' retorted our wise man, 'Do you think I'm a bleeding rajah? Here, *pakro ek rupiya*' (Here, take one rupee), and throwing the Rupee at him, he puffed his chest and strutted into the shelter of the Palladium, well pleased with the bargain!

Be warned though that not all bargains were as fair.

By the turn of the nineteenth century nearly all the houses belonged to officers, civil and military, who were absentee landlords, relying on local estate agents to manage the properties.

The same holds true today. But if an owner dies intestate, all hell breaks loose. The property changes hands several times, in seventeen shades of grey and in some places, the squatters are hard to winnow from the real inheritors.

Chapter 7

No Stealing Or Killing Please

Aago lage pachi khannu kuwa

NEPALI PROVERB

(To dig a well after a fire breaks out.)

You could say that by and large our hill station is a peaceful place where the main occupation of the police force is traffic control, protocol, escort or VIP duty, especially in the summer months. Yet there is no dearth of excitement.

What else can one say of our one and only nationalised bank robbery?

In the sleepy hollow of Jharipani, it was just like any other morning. The doors of the bank had barely opened. The new bank manager had joined duty a few days ago. He was at the desk while the teller straightened things. A hoarse voice whispered: 'Oy! Give me money!'

'Fill up the withdrawal form!' the teller said.

'Oy! Give me money!' The voice insisted.

The teller looked up—straight down the barrel of a gun. At the end of the gun stood a man in a hat, trench coat and dark goggles. Our town was witnessing its first bank robbery—Bollywood style!

Money in hand, the robber darted out of the bank and into a waiting taxi which he had, with amazing cupidity, hired from town as his getaway vehicle. It proved to be a grave mistake.

Arriving on the motor road, he most thoughtfully settled his dues with the taxi driver (who promptly drove back straight to the police station to report the robbery). Our bank robber waited on the road to catch a bus going down to the plains. I am told the policemen were convulsed in laughter, doubled up as it were, as they lay in wait for the bank robber to arrive at the toll barrier. During his interrogation, he revealed a cash flow problem induced, no doubt, by the exorbitant boarding fee he had to shell out for his two school going children.

Yes! Given the steep fee structures of our exalted Eton's of the East, some folks do resort to desperate measures.

Chunnu was the nickname of the protagonist of this tale, who, for the five decades and more of his charmed life likes to believe he's a busy hotelier. For the purposes of this tale, let us also call him by the nickname his parents so lovingly bestowed on him.

While it's true his greying hair gave him a distinguished air, the piles a concerned look but neither of these came to his help one rosy autumn morning when he saw an attractive dusky woman in tribal attire sashay up the ramp to the hotel, lift the latch off the gate to walk up to his doorstep. She was tall, dark, and comely, with a come hither look.

Yes! Things were really looking up!

'Humari gai aur mharo jana koh policewalon nay bandh kar diyo hai!' (The police have locked up our cows and my husband!), said the woman.

'Kahan?' (Where?), asked Chunnu solicitously, always ready to help a damsel in distress, especially if she was good looking.

'Raiwala mein!' (In Raiwala)

Raiwala is a sleepy old settlement on the railway line between Dehra and Hardwar. Most trains do not slow down, those that do, do so only briefly, hurrying off as if eager to get away.

Get away? Chunnu was not going anywhere. He was sold—hook, line and sinker.

'Paisay mangtey hain aur main yahan kissi koh nahin janti!' (They want money and I know no one here!), she added.

Pointing to a grungy pouch, she suggested pawning the silver therein as security for a temporary bridging loan. Of course she'd repay it from monies that came from the sale of milk and butter, once the cows and *mharo jana* (her husband) were freed from police custody.

'Don't you dare give her anything!' whispered Jaya, his wife.

But Chunnu belonged to the Land of Nod. He was not listening.

'Sahib! Doesn't sound right,' advised his manager, who'd been drawn by the commotion.

But Chunnu was transfixed.

He dressed up, as he always does, perfectly—cuff-links, tie, tie-pin, not forgetting the ubiquitous Rotary lapel-pin, and off he went to the bank, borrowed money, and came home to the swift exchange. It was almost a blur. The swag bag was his, the money went to the woman.

Years later, Chunnu's manager snickers: 'She took the money, gave sahib the jingling bundle and was off!' That was that.

When the satchel was moved to the privacy of the bedroom for safe-keeping in the family vault, Jaya suggested: 'Let's see what's in it.'

Like the devil's purse, when it was opened, they found nothing. There it lay—just worthless pieces of pewter strewn on the bed like burnt out dreams.

'We took off in all four directions,' remembers the manager, 'but by then she'd vanished into thin air!'

'We even went down to Raiwala but there was no trace of the cow, *mharo jana* or the police!' Jaya tells me.

All that was left behind was *'mharo jana'*—a lasting leitmotif to tease a smile out of Chunnu if you cross his path.

Our narrow makeshift lanes, are a collage of India, where regions, religions and races live together, jostling for space. If you peer through the mist of time, you'll find rogues and saints, crooks and innocents, everybody scrambling for a place in the weak winter sun. This is where folks meet, swap tales, exchange *gupp* and gossip (some false, others tinged with truth), part, sometimes never to meet again. This is where the pragmatism of the plains of North India clash, often head on, with the naivety of the hills.

Someone burgled the home of one of my gentler colleagues, an absent-minded professor, who had simply forgotten to lock the door while hurrying off to college.

'Thank you! Thank you so very much!' he gushed effusively to the local constabulary when they finally arrived.

'*Ajeeb shahar hai yeh!*' (What a strange town this!), complained constable Usman Zaidi, the police-van driver, as they investigated the break-in at the lonely cottage, muttering:

'*Jis koh dekho* thank you, thank you *kah deta hai! Array ghar jakar bachon koh kya dunga yeh* thank you, thank you?' (Whoever you meet, just says thank you, thank you, no one gives you money, what am I going to give to my children on going home? Just this thank you, thank you?)

'*Kisnay kaha tha itney duur jungle main ghar bananay koh?*' (Who told you to make a house so far away in the middle of a forest?)

'*Arrey hum bewakoof hain joh mohallay main rahtain hain?*' (Are we fools to live in colonies?), he rambled.

I guess that's as close to the truth one will ever get about our home in the hills. Everyone is polite, courteous and gentle to a fault. Get practical and you tend to walk straight into a wall. At least I did, when I gave a lift to a paunchy member of the police on his way to the court in the plains of Dehra down below.

As my old bike puttered downhill, I tried to make polite conversation: 'Not everyone on the force can possibly be on the take!' I ventured.

'Yes Sir!' he replied drawing a deep breath: 'When I joined the force, I was as straight as they come, determined to walk the straight and narrow. But my first leave was a cold homecoming to my village in the plains.

'What happened?' I asked.

'I had little money. I did take back a few trinkets, which everyone smirked at. So I turned to this wise old man, who had seen many summers. *Chacha* was a know-it-all!'

'What did he say?'

'Jab sab bheej raiyey toh tuh nay hee kyon chatta tanah hua?' (When everyone is getting drenched, why are you the only one with a taut umbrella?)

That constitutes the most pernicious argument I had ever heard for the perpetuation of corruption—if you can't fight them, join them.

Silence dominated the rest of our journey downhill, I knew I had done it again. I had firmly planted both my feet in my mouth.

Every few years, a magician turns up here, flashes money and proceeds to seduce the pants off the upper drawer. With the finesse of a con artist, he infiltrates their ranks, throws great parties, and charms the old biddies, seduces their off-springs with promises of pots of gold waiting at the end of the rainbow.

Then, one fine morning, he does the Bangkok-act—simply vanishes. Only much later folks find both their money and their daughters missing!

'He's just another stuffed shirt!' warned an old aunt. But who was listening when 'international tea taster' Rafiq Kidwai arrived in town like a jack-in-the-box, armed with an impressive gilt-edged degree from Yale University.

'Did he really go to Yale?' asked a visitor.

'Of course he did,' he was quickly reassured by a wise old man. 'A seven day course including a three day weekend tour of the countryside.'

With these tools of the trade, he wormed his way into the rarefied stratosphere of the town's upper crust. While 'taken in' does do justice, 'taken over' would be more like it. He invaded every house, dangled the bait and most took a greedy bite.

Please remember this scene is set in the austere socialist order of the late 1960s. One had just acquired a pair of 'bellbottoms' Apache jeans; 'Camlin' geometry box with Flora pencils; gave one's neighbour's phone number because you had booked your connection five years ago and it hadn't still come; phone calls were classified as ordinary, urgent and lightning; the family car was a Fiat or an Ambassador festooned with lace curtains, and the only gadgets were the black and white TV, the fridge and a solitary mixie.

Arrived into this Spartan world, he peddled dreams of walk-in fridges, fancy cars and luxury flats in far off Calcutta and Bombay.

'An imported General Electric fridge will be perfect for all those cold cuts—ham, salami, bacon!' he assured the credulous hotelier.

Silver leapt into his pockets.

'For you a white Mercedes Benz car Mr Puri!' he convinced the balding Mussoorie merchant.

The fat was in the fire. Silver leapt once again.

One morning, our charmer vamoosed, and not alone, gone with him too was the pretty wife of a local contractor.

But she was back three days later, looking flushed and happy, giggling: 'He was such a nice man.' She laid it on for those who'd wanted to listen to her story. 'It takes time to get all these things he's promised!'

Yes! It does take time—sometimes eternity, if not forever!

Mr Kidwai had gone, lost in the great greyness of India.

In his wake, came Mrs Cheehal, a femme fatale of the Matahari variety. She surfaced in town a sultry summer's evening, renting Macquarie Cottage. Word was out she had come from a family of rich planters in Kenya, wanting to buy a house in town.

She was attractive. She was willing. And willing most certainly were half the eager beavers in town. In no time, they were cluttering her front door.

Vying with each other, they lavished expensive gifts upon her. The gifts were not the problem. The brawls were. Noisy dog fights, that broke out amongst the long queue of suitors. One evening, one of them, finding the gate locked, sneaked over the wall. The lights in the cottage were on, but Mrs Cheehal was gone. She vanished with all the gifts bestowed upon her. All the lusting lovers searched far and wide but she had melted away into the night.

At the time of writing, there's a new kid on the block, an iron stuck in every fire, with no time for the hoi polloi, while the chatterati and the literati are, literally, eating out of his hands. Someday, when he's done the Indian rope trick and vanished, he'll leave behind a trail of folly you shall hear about. But I will leave that *gupp* and gossip for the writers of tomorrow!

At Hotel Brentwood, in the 1960s, no one batted an eyelid when a honeymooning couple checked in and the man checked in as Raj Kapoor. No one gave much attention to the fact that it happened to be the name of the legendary Bollywood actor—an oversight that caused a lot of bother. In the morning, the gardener rushed to the owner, gasping: 'Sir! The guest in room number 201 asked me to carry his wife down to the front lawn for some film shooting! What should I do?'

In turn, the mild-mannered owner Mr Sahani was greeted by the lilt of a song being enacted by the newly arrived guest. It was from Raj Kapoor's recently released film *Jis Desh Mein Ganga Behti Hai*:

> *Hoton pay sachai rahti hai, jahan dil main safai rahti hai,*
> *Hum us desh kay wasi hain jis desh mein Ganga behti hai!*
> (Where truth is on the lips, where the heart is clear,
> We live in the country where the Ganges flows.)

'Bring that stupid woman down!' the guest snapped his fingers at the hotel staff, adding: 'I have a shot to finish!'

Two, not one, local doctors were roused from their sleep. Understandably, they were not amused. Arriving bleary eyed, their prognosis was simple:

'He's gone nuts! Let's give him a sedative!'

But how does one get an actor, who believes he's *really* Raj Kapoor in the middle of a dance sequence, to lie down?

But Mr Sahani was a man for all reasons.

'Sir! The Director is waiting for the next shot in the room upstairs!' he said to our failed actor.

'Okay! Let me set my hair first,' said the man.

Luckily, the rest went like a dream. Silence please! Take one! Lights! Sound rolling! Camera! ACTION! Believing that it was a part of the script, our would-be hero lay down, and the sedative was administered. It worked. Our budding actor went off to sleep long enough to be bundled into a taxi by the wife's family who had arrived after a harrowing ten-hour journey to the hills.

I'm told on the drive back to Delhi, driving past the sugarcane fields, he would break out into song believing the camera was still rolling. All the while he lay down and sang the same very song again and again.

Of course, at times, some of our more sordid affairs are hushed up or simply brushed under the carpet. But you could hardly have done that with an incident that occurred at Zephyr Hall boarding house. On 25 July, 1927, at the height of the season, in the heart of the town, and in broad daylight, there occurred a double tragedy that certainly set the station agog. In a full boarding house, soon after midday, the boarders were startled when a shot rang out from one of the rooms and a woman screamed. Other shots followed in quick succession. Those in the public rooms, verandas, or outside, dived for safety into their own rooms and bolted the doors. One unhappy boarder, however, ignorant of where the desperate man with the gun might be at the moment, came around the corner with his arms well above his head taking no chances. As he turned a corner—and as luck would have it, he ran straight into the levelled pistol. Even the man who held it and had just killed his own wife, laughed!

You might laugh too, but say what you will, it was a delicate situation to face, for even the armed constabulary had to tread warily when they arrived.

Mr Owen had just shot his wife dead, wounded his daughter, and finally shot himself.

No story of crime and punishment in our hill station is complete without mention of the strange events at the Savoy hotel. This historic edifice is over a century old and in those long years, it's had a fair share of notoriety—though none like the Garnett Orme case.

On 18 October, 1911, in Suite number 8, the hotel staff discovered the body of Lady Francis Mary Garnett Orme, whose constant companion, Miss Mountstephen had left town several days ago.

The police suspected death by poisoning. A tumbler by the bedside was believed to smell of prussic acid.

The deceased had been in the habit of taking soda bicarbonate for a stomach ailment as a result of which the bottle had to be constantly replenished. To add to the mystery, in those hoary days of the Madame Blavatsky and the Theosophists, the two ladies were given to crystal gazing, séances, mesmerism and emanations from the psychic world. When the body was found, it seemed to have been laid out as if in preparation for the last rites. Had poison been administered and if death occurred by suicide, the body could not have lain in so 'comfortable' a position, however fast, or slow, the poison was.

Savoy Hotel.
Mussoorie.

The suite was bolted from inside when the body was discovered, though later a maidservant did swear that she had seen 'someone' (whom she could not identify) escaping through the skylight.

This statement solved the mystery of the bolted door but did little to solve this enigmatic case. Another line of action was therefore adopted—could the person who made the lethal draught have possibly made the concoction and be miles away by the time the fatal dose was taken?

Protracted investigation and legal proceedings followed because Miss Mountstephen was the executrix of Lady Garnett Orme's will. But the court refused to issue a probate of Letters of Administration. Miss Orme's brother, Mr Hunter Garnett Orme came out from England to contest the claim, which was decided in his favour on 12 October, 1912, by the district judge of Saharanpur.

Subsequent appeals by Miss Mountstephen before a two-judge bench in the Allahabad High Court were refused. She sailed back home and the attending doctor on the deceased lost a flourishing practice.

A weird sequel—if one may call it that—was the death nine weeks later of a decorative painter, Mr Charles John Jackson, a friend of several folks in the Garnett Orme saga. He too died rather suddenly, supposedly of cholera or something appearing like it.

A month later, someone suspected otherwise and when the body was exhumed, it was perfectly preserved!

Who killed Jackson? Arsenic poisoning was presumed. There were no suspects and the mystery was never solved. Such was the immense interest generated by the case that Rudyard Kipling wrote to Arthur Conan Doyle asking him to come out to India. But the creator of Sherlock Holmes never took up the offer and the case remained unresolved.

Exactly eighty years later, a tragedy unfolded in the same Suite number 8 where a professor accompanied by his wife and two physically challenged daughters checked into the hotel. Next morning, when they did not stir, the room boy presumed they must have overslept. But by noon, his forehead was creased. He told the lobby manager who in turn passed on the message to the front desk, which took some time in informing Chattar Singh Negi, the old manager of Savoy. Half a day had been wasted by the time the police force arrived.

The door was forced open. A stench of pesticide emanated from the room. On the floor, lay the lifeless bodies of the girls while the couple were discovered in the adjoining room, barely breathing—a suicide pact had gone awry. Timely help at a local hospital saved the couple's lives.

No one could save the lives of two sisters Raj and Upendra Dua, who owned a boutique in town. They were clobbered to death in Kalissa Cottage, in July 2006. There was no forced entry. No break in and nothing was missing. The crime was particularly brutal. Could it be the handiwork of one they had befriended? But then they were introverts, a bit aloof and had very few friends. The perpetrators are still at large.

Still roaming free are the intruders who arrived early morning at Oak Ville, home to the Alter family. Ameeta, author Stephen Alter's wife, aroused from her sleep by their incessant knocking, presumed it must be someone looking for odd jobs. She opened the door to four masked men, who rudely pushed her aside, forcing their way into the house insisting on being taken to the family safe.

Unfortunately the house had no safe!

Stumbling into the scene, bleary eyed, Steve walked straight into the armed robbers to be brutally attacked with a knife. Good luck, god's grace and the dedication plus skill of the mission hospital doctors saved the young author's life. For that we are all grateful.

The attackers are still at large.

In one of our hotels, the drunk canteen manager snuffed out the life of one of his helpers, buried him in the floor of one of the rooms and then re-laid the concrete. As luck would have it, the cement he used was spurious. A strong smell emanating from the room led to the corpse being exhumed.

Dead men do tell tales in our sleepy little town.

Yet, let us not dwell too long on these tragedies but think instead of the hundreds of thousands who come up the hill in high spirits and leave in good spirits—a cocktail of mountain air, stunning views and aided no doubt by a drop or two of real spirits.

Chapter 8

What's In A Name

Kitlu karey gurah key sau, takney-takney maur
GARHWALI PROVERB

(The worm copies the snake and dies wriggling.)

What's in a name? Quite a bit if you go by successive waves of migrants who flocked from the hinterlands of the Garhwal Himalayas, to the station looking for work. The Scottish and Irish names that the pioneers had given their abodes in the hills must have been tongue twisters.

What would you make of names like 'Cefn Cord' or 'Brandlesome'? They found it simpler to call one 'Company-khud' and the other 'Bindal-Sone'—after the two rivers in the valley—or similar changes of name.

In their combined wisdom, for purely practical reasons, the hill folk set out to shape and reshape the names of the properties. At the old bus terminus, your luggage was whisked away by the coolies, who would say: *Dhangwali* or the 'one on the precipice' for Prospect Point; *Banjwali* aptly described the dense clump of oaks surrounding Tabor; *Daatwali* evoked the via-duct like approach to Redburn Estate, and St Asaph's didn't mean anything to the locals and much to the owner's disgust it became *sandass* (latrine)! Some of these names have sunk without a ripple, and as I write, quite a few names cling on to the older properties.

Hampton Court Convent is still called the *Calcuttiya School* in everlasting memory of those frugal nuns, who, in the nineteenth century, made the long journey up the Ganga in a boat from Calcutta to the hills. Waverley Convent remains *Kala School*, a tribute to the nun's black habits. The East India Company lends its name to two institutions, Woodstock School and the Municipal Gardens, which are even now known as the *Company School* and the *Company Bagh.*

Wynberg School along the old bridle path was originally a hotel owned by a certain Bobby Heseltine and came to be known as *Bobby Sahib ka hotel.* Later, as a school it simply became *Bobby Sahib ka School.*

This frenzy of renaming saw Childer Castle's barred windows turning its name into *Seekhwali Kothi.* One had grown up believing that Sister's Bazaar was named after the nursing sisters working at the British Military Hospital! It was my turn to be surprised to learn that *Jodi Bungla* or the twin bungalows at the mouth of the market, where a new road bisects the two homes, gave it its name. And the old bungalow, *Chirdyawali* or the house of birds, took its name from the aviary full of budgerigars. Their chirping could be heard on the motor road nearby.

Another puzzle was Maryville Estate in Barlowganj, home to generations of the old Foster family, cousins of the famous Skinners, which my father called *Phooswali* or the house with a thatch roof. Last year, a friend sent me some old photographs of our town taken in the late 1860s. Suddenly the mystery was solved—all our homes were thatch-covered. It was, perhaps a good choice in the British Isles—but a bad one in the Indian monsoon. Maryville was the last die-hard to retain a thatched roof.

Apparently Seaforth Lodge was called *Sirphodi Lodge* or the House of the Skull-bashers because of the constant squabbling among the folks who once lived there.

Or take Eastwood, which housed a dairy where they made butter. Later the buttermilk was emptied down the drains, giving it the name *Doodhwali Kothi* or the House of Milk.

Why would Prospect Lodge, at the end of Sister's Bazaar be called *Naharwali* or the House of the Canal? There are no remnants of a canal or even the faint memories of water. This time around, I owe it to the memory of Mr Inder Prakash, old-time resident and owner of A Prakash & Co, who told me: 'There used to be a spring here till the Uttarkashi earthquake of 1995, then the mountain moved, or landslide silenced the gurgling sound forever.'

Other houses were not so lucky. They were named after their owners and there were no genteel niceties extended. Just too bad if the owner happened to be afflicted by some deformity, which were picked upon by the boys in the bazaars. Soon, one had names like *Langreywali Kothi* or the House of the Lame Man, *Tundi-ki-Kothi* or the House of the One Armed Lady, and even *Lal Muuhwali Kothi* or the House of the Red-faced Lady.

This renaming of properties was not just restricted to the vernacular. Let us take for example the old and famous Charleville hotel. Elsewhere in the world, the correct pronunciation would have been 'Sharly-ville', but in this instance it would be incorrect. It was named after the two sons of the banker, Mr Hobson—Charlie and Willie—the locals still call it *Charlie-Billie.*

On the way to school, one would meet old *langra*-Powell or lame-Powell at the Seven Oaks, along the old Kipling Road, the homestead of the famous Powell family, which owned vast tracts of the Doon valley. He had a repertoire of nonsensical Anglo-Indian rhymes:

Duum duum duum,
Bakri ka duum,
Hum khain gosth,
Tum khao duum.

Or his version of Humpty Dumpty:

Hamti Damti charhgaya chatt,
Hamti Damti girgaya phatt,
Raja ki paltan, Rani key ghorey,
Hamti Damti kabhi nah jodey.

Circa 1950s... As a five-year old, I would arrive at the intimidating gates of Grace Mount Estate near the Library, home to Rai Bahadur Lachman Das, clutching my father's coat. We would be ushered into his august presence in a dark room where he squatted on a large mattress on the ground. In the embalmed darkness, the only way you could tell that he was actually there was when he'd move his eyeballs.

Sethji, as the well-off were addressed in those days, was a superstitious man given to the occult sciences, astrology, numerology and gems. With rapt attention, I heard the stories of how he had bought a diamond ring in Lucknow's Hazratganj and ill luck ensued! Hardly had he reached the gates of his mansion on AP Sen Road, news trickled in of a boiler exploding in one of his numerous sugar mills. 'I didn't even get out of the car. I went straight back to the jewellers and plonked the stone before him!'

'Saili *sa'ab!*' he warned my father: 'Never ever wear a precious stone without first testing it! Pure bad luck.'

'Yes! *Sethji*!' nodded my father bravely for someone who had barely two coins to rub together; here he had to listen to tales of buying gems.

As we'd get up to leave, *Sethji* would rummage his crumpled pockets. Out would pop a copper coin, which he'd slowly raise up to his eyes. If it had a hole, he'd peer through it, just to make sure it wasn't anything more than a paisa. Then with a sigh it'd be given to me.

But if he couldn't see through it, it'd be worth a little more, so back into his pocket it went—a fresh round of hunting began. The old skinflint would have given any miser a run for his money, despite all his gems.

Gems and money left in trust in our banks has had a chequered history. The North-West Bank, our first bank, was floated in 1836 and came to grief in 1842. Seventeen years later the Delhi and London Bank opened in 1859 and was followed by the Mansuri Savings Bank in 1864. A certain Mr F Moss (after whom Mossy Falls is named!) launched the Himalaya Bank which collapsed in 1884, followed by the crashes of the Bank of Upper India, the Alliance Bank and the Himalaya Bank.

Of the last, it is rumoured that those 'in the know' knew that the bank was about to go bust, were aware of a new client they accepted at so precarious a time. To its everlasting shame, on the eve of its collapse, it accepted the life savings of an old man and caused him to die of a broken heart.

But I don't think my father was shattered when the bank went bust, not if you go by the old stub of his tattered Bhagwan Das Bank's cheque-book, which I found among his papers years later in our attic. Balance, just Rs 169. No such luck awaited Seth Chander Sain, the owner of the Mansaram Bank, whose timely heart attack, came just two days before the bank folded up. Death saved him from the ignominy of going bankrupt. There are times when I wonder if the great banker had ever looked down from his six-floor pent house. If he had, he could not have missed the young lad sitting in a patch of sunshine on the road trying to finish his home-work. He certainty would not even in his wildest dreams, have foreseen that the industrious little boy, would one day become a leading lawyer and later, a Member of Parliament, or that when his bank crashed, the government would appoint him as the Official Receiver of all the Bank's properties—Summer House, Mullingar Estate, Mansaram Cricket and many more.

Ours was one of the earliest Municipalities in India, constituted in 1842. Starting from a tiny room in the Kutchery, it remains a lightning conductor for the citizen's ire.

'That is just our own little house owning scheme,' Mrs A, our local *Happy Valley Express* will tell anyone willing to listen.

And our city fathers, like politicians elsewhere, love seeing their names etched on to foundation stones for projects, both big and small. You'll see these marble and granite plaques on railings, gates, public offices, almost everything except bathrooms! If you go looking for them years later, you'll find them littering the hillside in various states of disarray.

Take for instance, the imposing sandstone monolith listing the founding fathers of the local municipal college when it came into being in the 1960s and went missing soon after. That is until one day I found some Nepalese labourers, outside their hutments abutting the college, using it most aptly to grind their coriander-green chilli chutney! They gave me a lick of the chutney. It tasted good. Finally, at long last, someone had spiced up the fast fading names of the town's long forgotten sons.

'In an abandoned village, the mouse shall be king!' Father said.

Fame is a deceiving elf, here today, gone tomorrow, and though our names may be carved in stone, they might as well have been writ on water.

Opposite the old Library, they built an ungainly concrete gate in the 1960s; forty years later it had become a bottleneck. It was pulled down without as much as by-your-leave, while a statue of Mahatma Gandhi, at the centre of town square was pushed into a corner. Cars have become the steeds of our New Age gods. Later the Town Hall crumbled in a cloud of dust and now our Clock Tower has gone missing too!

Around the same time, the rosy-cheeked, nimble footed sirens of the Ruby wine shop on the Mall, caused many a ship-wreck, leaving a trail of shattered hearts. It wasn't on account of those who visited the shop. Those who tippled, went in, bought their daily quota and slunk away. The teetotallers were the problem—like a murder of crows, they congregate to perch on the railings opposite the shop—to get a glimpse of the owner's stunning daughters who lived in a flat near the shop—six of them, each prettier than the other!

Over the years, one by one, the girls settled down. The crows took flight leaving the 'wailing railings' forever!

Soon after the Ruby wine shop became unstuck.

Resuscitated, albeit briefly, it turned into a store for woollens—but those glad rags were no match for the warmth of the real thing.

It's that kind of place our home in the hills. Little is sacred. Nothing lasts forever. Only the Himalayas remain permanent reminders in an impermanent world.

Chapter 9

Our Match Fixing

Balakoh koh haath aur budhya koh gicha khujlaundu randdhu

GARHWALI PROVERB

(A child's hands and an old man's mouth are always itching.)

February and March 1959: News crackled over the static of All India Radio from Lhasa. Reports trickled in of clashes between the Chinese troops and the militias of His Holiness the Dalai Lama. A week or so later, he resurfaced near Kalimpong to arrive in these foothills on 9 March, 1959, to spend his first night here at Birla House.

The place was festooned with fluttering prayer flags to become home to the large Tibetan diaspora. Among the many refugees was Kunga Lodey and his large family, who pioneered handmade noodles from his home in the old Mullingar ruins.

Where would he sell these? All the sceptics clucked.

But the last laugh was on us. We could not have got it more wrong, as the hillside missionaries became his first customers and today, Tibetan cuisine

has come into its own with every shack, big or small, serving a moveable feast where you can wash the noodles down with liberal serving of *chang*, the Tibetan rice-beer and *pai,* the mustard seed wine.

As I write, one cannot attend a wedding in Garhwal which does not serve chow mien!

'At this rate,' an old timer tells me, '...it's now the chief dish of Uttarakhand!'

Abutting this refugee settlement, overpowering it, almost choking it, rise the towering buildings of the Lal Bahadur Shastri National Academy of Administration housed on the grounds of the old Charleville hotel. Records tell us, in late 1950s, things were not going too well for these hills. Their floundering economy, with a twenty per cent occupancy, spelled disaster, and the government adroitly acquired the hotel for a proverbial song—*just* Rs 8 lakhs! And the Administrative Academy moved from Metcalfe House to the hills. Along with it came many a legend. Among these is the tradition of the faculty inviting the new officers for a chit-chat over tea, lunch or dinner to their homes. A steno to one of the deputy directors was asked to make out the formal invitations. This he proceeded to do with gusto.

'Always check his damn drafts,' said an outgoing bureaucrat to the other. 'Once on one of my dinner invitation, under dress code he wrote: Optional.'

'What's that supposed to mean?' I quizzed him, horrified that everyone was being asked to come in the buff to a Full Monty party.

He gave me a withering look: 'Sir! If the dress code is optional, instead of formal, they can wear anything they like. No?'

Having left behind them the euphoria of clearing one of the toughest exams in the country, the young probationers, find themselves deposited at the gates of the Academy, only to discover that each entrant is as bright if not brighter than their compradors. The only give-away are the clothes—ill-fitting safari suits represent small town or rural Bharat while city slickers stick out like sore thumbs—the bold, brave and brash yuppies have Wrangler jeans, Reebok shoes, Polo T-shirts and Dolce & Gabbana shades. Don't worry, soon the attitude level drops to that of eighteen year olds going back to college.

Go looking for them a week later, after the blender of training, packed from dawn to dusk, with jogging, physical training and back-to-back classes on diverse subjects ranging from land reforms to officer-like-qualities, and differences have begun to vanish. Bharat has merged with India, in formal black suits. Make no mistake, they've all perfected the art of sleeping through their classes, eyes wide open!

'The civil services were based on impartiality, integrity, honesty and no bending to any pressure, no deviation from the path of justice,' speaker after speaker will exhort the youngsters.

'Those stalwarts disappeared. Politicization of the services started. What made them give up? Simple! The power to transfer, to suspend or deny desired postings. The attitude turned into if you can't lick them, join them. Remember this is an "other-regarding" service, not a "self-regarding" one. Otherwise, if you want to make money, leave now and go into the corporate world!'

Few leave. Most stay, putting up with the charms of *shishtachar* (etiquette) classes where one is taught the basics of social behaviour. They are introduced to things like *The Warrant of Precedence* with its many pages of closely packed print. All it does is, it teaches one who stands where in the pecking order. For instance, where would you seat an Inspector of Tolls in relation to a junior Health Officer at an official dinner?

At one such grand dinner an officer trainee, quizzed the course coordinator: 'Sir! I suppose in such a large dining hall it is difficult to know how to place people?'

'Not at all,' the course coordinator assured him. 'Usually, the people who matter don't mind and the people who mind don't matter!'

Please take this with a pinch of salt for the order of seating is as important as the rungs of a ladder and anyone who breaks the rules is assured a sharp rebuke. Miss Pretty, a young officer trainee breezed gaily in with one of the senior deputy directors at her first formal dinner. Later in one of the washrooms, Mrs Inscrutable, wife of one of the senior Deputy Directors, accosted her and said: 'I know you're new and have not been here very long, but you will remember that single women do not go to a formal dinner before married ladies!'

So, the only constant here is change, and every batch is assured its quota of the Keen Type Probationers, known in academy parlance as KTPs, who concentrate purely on academics while giving the fun and games a miss. They go through the foundation course like a car going uphill with a sputtering engine, missing out on the scenery.

Interestingly, there is a lot of 'match fixing' here—it would put to shame any of those shady bookies in cricket's great game. No sooner are the results of the state-wise cadre allotment out, all hell breaks loose. Friendships formed during the course are shattered on the shoals of cadre-based pragmatism. Those headed for hot spots begin to make eyes at the ones who have got more peaceful places. Generally, you could say that you end up in a mix of the CBMs (Cadre-Based Marriages) and DBMs (Dowry Based Marriages). Alas! Love, usually, flounders on the jagged reefs of reality.

If not mates, what these youngsters do take with them is the bonding among batch mates. The physical training's shrill whistle, the jog to Library, the Himalayan treks, the village-visits and nostalgia of cultural bashes are things that will not fade. These last forever!

Or do they? I wondered especially after I met the forty-something year old Palden Gyatso Tenzing, of the Kerala cadre, who'd hung up his boots to swap his career in the civil services for a long trip home to Sikkim.

Astride his shiny Bullet Thunderbird motorcycle, he roared up the incline to our home, with cadre mate TK Manoj Kumar riding pillion. He had just touched base with his roots in the Academy. This was where it had all begun.

Yes! He definitely was your odd man out for he had finally broken loose.

'I am following my heart. It was sickening to work under bosses who ought to be shooed, and I had to "Sir" the dopes too!' he told me.

In his book *Don't Ask Any Old Bloke for Directions*, he wrote: 'It was a great day for me when I met the legendary Ruskin Bond in Ganesh Saili's home. Ruskin still has a twinkle in his eyes when he talks sexy, even at his age. I can imagine the blaze in his youth.'

Our home, dear reader, has often, cattily, been called the Grand Central Station—where all kinds of people surface to pass through—from celebrities to con artists, it has survived them all and when I saw Tenzing with his tousled hair, even my pets, Kaali and Bhuri knew this one was special.

As the sun began to set, I brought out some liquid sustenance, and he whispered in my ear: '*Sir*! Please let *me* make Mr Bond a drink. Someday I'll be able to brag to my grandchildren that I poured a drink for the Grand Old Man of the Mountains!'

Poor Tenzing never could show off to anyone. A few months later, he passed away of a sudden illness in Gangtok.

My friend, you'll always be missed in this little corner of the planet!

West of the Academy opposite Benog hill, is the old resort of Cloud End. This forgotten corner was once home to a host of famous men—Sir George

Everest, Surveyor-General; William Fraser, the Resident of Delhi and the owner of Leopard Lodge, and Major Swetenham, the Commandant of the Invalids Establishment.

How the Major came to own the estate is the stuff of fairy-tales. Out hunting with his companions, he was enchanted by the song of a local hill girl gathering fodder for her cows. Trailing her home, he discovered she was the daughter of one of the local village chiefs. She was all of fourteen, he twenty years older. But Cupid had struck. Swept off his feet, he begged her father to allow him to marry her. A little later, she became Mrs Swetenham—the matriarch of a great family.

Old time resident, the late Jim Keelan, once told me: 'One of the Swetenhams was so beautiful, so blemishless, that the family had a deaf and dumb servant who walked ahead of her as she went for a walk, and, on seeing a stranger approaching, he swept the road with a large broom, raising clouds of dust on the path ahead which he continued to do till the passer-by had gone past. For the family did not want any evil eye falling upon her.'

If for a moment I could walk you to the top of Benog hill, you might as well acquaint yourself with another legend—the elusive bird—the Mountain quail (*Ophrysia superciliosa*), which was reportedly last seen in the area.

Is it extinct or elusive? Ornithologists differ.

Last sighted in this area in November 1865 in a hollow between Bhadraj and Benog peak, at an elevation of about 6,000 feet, the bird has not been spotted here since.

Jharipani at 5,500 feet seemed a haunt of the bird. In 1867, three persons, one a hunter and two naturalists saw these birds here and wrote about them. Kenneth Mackinnon, your average *shikari*, shot several of them, later he recalled he had only heard of them coming around in winter.

A certain Captain Hutton reports they were scurrying around his home in Jharipani between 1867 and 1868. The last person to see two birds alive was Major Carwithen and he was just your dumb hunter who shot the female of the pair!

Locals believe the Mountain quail migrated from Central Asia to India—probably a denizen of some of the eastern portions of Tibet. These thinly populated areas are so rarely explored that a bird given to reclusive habits, fond of steep, grassy slopes, when disturbed, scurry between the tall grass rather than fly or hide, to escape detection.

I for one won't be surprised if some day they return, perhaps when the climatic conditions are the same as they were in 1867 or 1868. Till that happens, I'm afraid you'll have to be content with the ten stuffed specimens scattered in museums around the world!

Chapter 10

Acts Of The Gods

Marich cauri parcha aphnai tejle
NEWARI PROVERB

(The pepper is wrinkled by its own heat.)

At 7,000 feet, lust has often led to fires of one kind, we've mostly been spared the devastating fires that have wiped out the old buildings of Shimla. It could be because our homes were built of the slow burning rhododendron and oak while theirs were of the resinous pines.

'The Wynberg Homes' including Bala Hisar seems to have been particularly vulnerable to flames. In 1886, Mrs Barton-West started it in Rockville, with just two pupils, Peter and Mary Cables. In the basement of the building was a wood charcoal kiln which exploded without injury to anyone. It was considered prudent for the school to move to nearby Abbotsford and Dunedin on the Castle Hill estate, before finally settling down on the twin spurs of Bala Hisar. In the 1890s, the fine bungalow called Constantia Hall burnt down. Arson was suspected but nothing was proved.

On 29 March, 2009, an electrical short circuit started a blaze that reduced Wynberg-Allen's thousand-seat school auditorium to ashes. Starting at night, the blaze hurt no one. Phoenix-like it has risen from the ashes with firebreaks, sprinklers and state-of-the-art safety systems.

The Standard Skating Rink, which came up on the site of the glorious Stifles Restaurant in the 1940s was a great rendezvous for lovers. That is if you could put up with the music—just three 78 rpm records would play day in and day out, 365 days a year: *The Baby Elephant March, the Spanish Gypsy* and *the BlueDanube.*

Change was in the air. The grace of offering profuse apologies if you merely brushed past someone lasted till the 1960s; in the 1970s it became: 'What the hell were you there for if you can't knock down a few girls on the skating-floor?' Oftener than not, it led on to squabbles, that turned into street-battles spilling on to the roads.

Unsung, an age had moved on.

On it's ground floor, Guruji's Chitrashala displayed paintings of the town's luminaries of the 1960s rubbing shoulders with those great leaders of the Indian National Movement.

Among his better-known works was the plywood cut-out of Capt Kirpa Ram Jauhar, which, for years after his passing, continued to greet visitors to Nandu's cottage. Mysteriously, in a case of instant self-combustion, it was destroyed soon after the establishment changed hands.

Those in the know tell me that once a fading beauty, a certain Mrs M, turned up to commission Guruji to paint a portrait of her. Her brief was simple: 'Add on a lot of jewellery. You know a pearl necklace, emerald earrings and a couple of priceless rubies too!'

'But *behenji* you're not wearing any of those!'

'Yes! I know,' she sighed, 'How I wish I was! You see my old man's having an affair. I know he'll marry her once I'm dead. I want the damn witch to go crazy looking for them once I'm gone!'

But it was not to be. On 17 April, 1968, the first floor Skating Rink was getting a lick of paint, as it always had, just before the tourist season, when a fire broke out in the evening. Fed by paint, spirit, varnish and turpentine, it raged through the night, reducing this fine building to a smouldering hulk by dawn. The proprietor's wife, trapped in her first-floor quarters, succumbed to the conflagration. Rumours abounded, spreading faster than the fire itself. Could it be that he'd insured his spouse recently or was it a fire insurance fraud? No one ever found out.

Though everyone found out when news came in of a fire at Rushbrook the residence of Dr AN Jha, the first director of the Administrative Academy. Popular lore has it that he was in the midst of a meeting and rushed off to the place, on the Mall, very distressed, convinced that fire would ravage everything especially his personal stash of vintage wines. He lowered his considerable bulk into a chair, lit up a pipe, but only after the treasure trove had been secured, safe and sound, by the officer trainees.

Unfortunately, this could not happen in May 1984, when fire starting in the kitchen of the old hotel (by then the Academy) destroyed the VIP guest room, the library (located right above the Mess), the dining room and the Director's residence for the last time!

And whoever said lightning never strikes the same place twice, would not have dared uttered those words if they had heard of the story of a Burnt Hill, which is variously, referred to as Witch's Hill or Pari Tibba (the Hill of Fairies). The place still has traces of some early ruins.

It is believed these ruins are the work of djinns, others claim that the spot has been repeatedly hit by lightning, attracted by the phosphate deposits on the hill.

Local lore has it that a high-ranking official found himself enmeshed in the clutches of a greedy moneylender and to extricate himself from the mire, he forced his daughter to marry the old fogey. Of course, much to the disgust of the young girl and her handsome suitor, posted at the Landour army depot. Years had passed, yet their ardour brought them together one last time.

Our Shylock was down in the plains when he heard the news. He turned around and headed straight back home to the hills. The couple decided to do what they should have done years ago—elope! A decision was made to avoid the main bridle path (where Shylock would have been) and use the goat tracks instead.

A sudden summer squall forced the lovers to seek safety and shelter in the ruins. Fate decreed lightning to strike the same spot again, and so it was. Echoes of the unrequited love linger around the lover's final resting place on Burnt Hill, which is hit by lightning many times.

The old *gupp* and gossip has it that the early victims of the Pari Tibba tragedy, similarly struck by lightning were relatives of a Capt Spread, who was killed in the same way. Strange that it seemed to follow the family and snuff out those who dare live in the hills. Capt Charles Henry Deane Spread of the Invalid Establishment was struck by lightning and killed at Bala Hisar on 3 September, 1879, as he collected rainwater from the drainpipes to develop some photographic plates. Strangely enough, twenty-four years later, on the very same day, 3 September, 1903, a bolt of lightning killed Miss Eleanor Amy Nunn, the Captain's cousin, a teacher in the Abbey School as she walked up to bolt the door in a storm.

Years later, another building in Bala Hisar was similarly struck, but luckily the principal had gone off to the cinema and lived to tell the tale. A raging fire almost levelled our local bazaar on 5 May, 1935, and the Municipal Board bought its first small, manual fire extinguisher. Its bulky size restricted movement and it was of little use when later the original Phoenix Lodge, burnt down to the ground after a hot air balloon from a wedding party settled on its thatched roof and the lumbering behemoth could not make it up the hill.

Tragedy struck on a warm summer night in May 1996, at the Parsonage—home to the Banerjees. Two wires of the service line, swayed by a strong breeze, short-circuited and the resultant sparks, hastened by a squall, set the home aflame. Once again, the fire engine could not get past the parked cars cramming the narrow lanes. Despite valiant fire fighting by all his neighbours, not much could be saved.

As Victor stood surveying the smouldering heap in the morning, a passerby asked commiseratively, 'Is there anything I can do to help?'

'Yes', Victor answered. 'You know anybody who wants to buy charcoal?', he said, totally detached after the disaster.

In a never-say-die spirit, the Banerjee's rebuilt their home—prettier than the last and is a tribute to the couple's indomitable courage.

Chapter 11

Moutain Lore

Apney Ganga kway undoh nahayo ubhoh nahayo

GARHWALI SAYING

(When the Ganga is yours, bathe upstream or downstream.)

If you walk past the Clock Tower, ignoring the road that goes on towards the Mall, but take instead the one that brought up the early visitors to the hills, you will stumble upon a clump of trees. Look through the gate and you will see the faint outlines of an old bungalow.

This was Woodlands School many moons ago. Not teeming with students, but only twenty of us. Please don't go looking for it today. It's gone. What remains are echoes of the poet Frost's lines:

There is a house,
That is no more a house,
Upon a farm that is no more a farm,
In a town that is no more a town.

Sixty years ago, the two sisters, Doris and Edith had a school to run. Later, in the 1960s, they closed the school down before retiring. Edith left to meet her Maker just a few days short of her hundredth birthday. On our last meeting she recalled: 'The school began at the Dingle, on the other side of the Clock Tower, but it didn't have a playing field, and so we moved to Woodlands with our father in 1905.'

It was here, that we as children, wandered around the vast estate, peering through dusty window-panes into abandoned rooms piled high with desks, benches and double-decker beds from another time—when this was a flourishing boarding-school.

What did she remember of the time gone by? 'Oh! Lots of picnics, card games, flower shows, dog shows and lot of fun,' she told me, adding: 'You know St Emilian's Church at the top of the hill? It had a Bishop called Brother Julius Caesar who'd ride to Church on a great white horse and give fiery sermons, full of brimstone and fire!' I had brought along my collection of old pictures of the town. I showed them to her. 'Oh! Those are TA Rust's pictures taken around 1890. No! I didn't know him, but his son Julian had such a lovely collection of butterflies. Wonder where his butterfly collection went?'

What remains is the gnarled medlar tree we used to climb as children. Simon, the parrot who screeched 'good morning' to us as we came in through the school's gate, is gone too. Instead of masses of petunias, geraniums, fuchsias and gladioli, the garden is overgrown. Litter from slummy hotels overflows on to the green grounds. Debris from the foundations of a newer guesthouse cascades down the hill on to the field below.

Old Mr AH, who retired from the railways in Saharanpur, and his family, took care of Edith in the last years of her life, and continue to live in one of the smaller cottages.

Gone too from another set of rooms in the corner of Woodlands, is Major-General N Ram of the nursing services, the only Indian recipient of the Param Vishisht Sewa Medal and the Florence Nightingale Award for distinguished service. Her abiding faith saw her travel around the mountains to the far-flung clinics set up by various Christian missions in Uttarakhand.

As I was about to leave during my last visit to Woodlands, a rosy-ringed parakeet shrieks in the medlar tree, bringing back memories of another day.

Every traveller to the hill station does not get to see the sleepy little hollow of Barlowganj which lies on the abandoned bridle path to Rajpur.

Its most imposing edifice, Sikander Hall now inhabited by Lilian Singh, the late Col Michael Skinner's sister, has been home to generations of the Skinner family, beginning with Colonel James Skinner, the patriarch of this Anglo-Indian dynasty, after whom the legendary Skinner's Horse is named. This irregular cavalry with their scarlet turbans, silver-edged girdles, black shields and bright yellow tunics were a mercenary force with the Marathas and the Mughals, before finally throwing in their lot with the John Company.

A Scotsman married a Hindu princess, and started a cosmopolitan trend the rest of his descendants followed. He was a larger than life character, who lived the life of a grand nawab, and preferred being called: Nasir-ud-Dowlah Colonel James Skinner Bahadur Ghalib Jung.

He built St James Church in old Delhi as a tribute to his faith, where in a final act of atonement, he willed his remains to be interred in front of the altar so that 'all men may step over his grave!'

But that's another story for another time.

Nobel Laureate Rudyard Kipling arrived here in 1888 and stayed at the Charleville hotel. But all he left us about Mussoorie are just four lines inscribed on a photograph in the front office:

And there were men with a thousand wants,
And women with babes galore,
But the dear little angels in Heaven know,
That Wutzler never swore.

And pray, who on earth was Wutzler? Well! It turns out he was the proprietor of the sprawling hotel, whose foul mouth would send his staff scurrying.

Then there were the Thatcher family who reputedly owned most of western Dehradun but by the beginning of the 1960s, they'd arrived to the end of the line—at least in Mussoorie.

Bit by bit, piece by piece, from the curtain-rings to the carpet, the *kabariwala*'s (ragpicker) bought the family's heirlooms and before Miss Thatcher, the last light of Rosemary Cottage near Waverley, was extinguished, her younger brother, Mr Deley came out of England to settle the estate.

But between the proverbial two monsoons, his frail constitution was no match for the onerous task at hand. As he shuttered himself down in the homestead, all sorts of do-gooders appeared at the door. Tragically, almost all of them got him to sign on blank papers.

Very soon, every other person was the beneficiary to the estate of the Thatchers. Interestingly, after he passed on, as many as seventeen people filed for probate. Predictably, the court threw out all the doctored wills, vesting the estate with the Custodian General.

Who got what? You might wonder.

Just clammy palms. All got precious little for all their valiant efforts.

At the other end of the town, above the old Bandstand, where once kisses were auctioned (in the 1920s) for charity, lived Anand Jauhar, or Nandu to his friends, who once owned the Savoy hotel. Well known for his repertoire of risqué jokes, he has seen it all—from owning the Indira restaurant in the Marble Arch, London, to the old Fonseca (now the Taj Mansingh) in Delhi. As one wag put it:

From Mussoorie to Bangalore,
Delhi to Lahore,
He's cracked his jokes galore!

In our small town, the Savoy bar was much more than a watering hole—it was a place where locals met travellers and sometimes, lasting friendships were forged.

Over the years, at the bar we met many interesting people—actors, authors, journalists, diplomats, drunks, cops and bureaucrats (serving, retired and on re-treading). Even Vishal Ohri, our nature loving bank manager, was one of our companions, as were the handsome young Maharajah of Alwar and his beautiful wife Ambika, the ever-youthful Karanwals, the ever-helpful Vibha and Surjit Das and of course, PK Mohanty, who as the District Magistrate, is reputed to have taken Bill Clinton by the hand to all the hotspots of Agra!

Though a lot of people who went through the Writers' Bar at Savoy look pretty far gone and sometimes it was hard to distinguish the living from the dead. But the real ghosts were those who managed to slip away without ever paying for their drinks.

Ruskin Bond and I didn't have to slip away. In the ten or twelve years during which we have helped prop up the place, we have seldom paid for a drink. That's the kind of friend we had in Nandu. One won't find a harsh word about him in our writing.

Mr Bakshi, one of the hotel managers, was a great sponge, but he never paid for a drink ever, because for twenty long years, he had a free run of the place while Nandu chased mirages overseas. Things came to such a pass that on one occasion, a guest at the hotel approached Nandu, asking: 'Sir! Are you Mr Bakshi, the manager?'

'Definitely not!' said Nandu with a straight face, adding: 'But the way things are going downhill, I'll soon be!'

Luckily for Nandu, Mr Bakshi put in his papers and moved on.

But this left Nandu on his own, as the summer season came and hotel tariffs had to be printed. A rush job had to be done by one of the old ram-shackled printing presses in town.

The printer's devil played havoc with interesting results instead of 'Ballroom with nightly dancing with band and cabaret', it had: '*Bathrooms* with nightly dancing with band and cabaret!'

In the good old days of the Savoy, up until the 1960s, Rudy Cotton was busy at the piano in the Savoy, while down the road, across the Mall,

Pat Blake and his twelve boys, held live music shows at Hakman's Grand hotel and the famous Thunderbird, Ashwani Kumar crooned at Whispering Windows restaurant. Sadly, though we did not know it then, the time of live music was fast coming to an end with the advent of the jukebox.

However, for over twenty years, up until the 1980s, the three hotels, Savoy, Hakman's and Whispering Windows organised lavish beauty contests. As old time resident, Narendra Sahani wistfully remembers: 'The Queen of Hills would turn into the Hill of Queens!"

'You could call them anything!' remembers Nandu, adding: 'Choose anything you like from Miss Mussoorie, Summer Queen, May Queen, Autumn Queen and if the names ran out, there was always space in the calendar for a round of Jungle Queen!'

And there was 'match fixing' here too! A long time before the expression had entered modern lexicon. The 'standard operating procedure' involved the organisers pointing out to the judges, in advance, the local magistrate's wife, who, despite her pear-shaped 32-40-50 figure, was to be the winner!

I saw it all fresh one summer's night. 1985 saw the last beauty queen contest in town. In hindsight, one could see why the last 'Savoy Queen' was doomed from the start. The drumbeat reached a crescendo; the lights dimmed to reveal Luscious Lola, a fast fading cabaret artist from Calcutta, who'd seen many summers, fluttering through the crowd. Barely had she thrown her skirt at a greying geezer, the winner of the third prize was announced. Mrs Sundri, wife of a local *dhaba*-owner, by miles the prettiest lady in the ballroom, heard her name. She was stunned, her husband shocked. Livid at his wife coming last, he jumped on to the stage ahead of her and kicked the offending prize, a black and-white TV clean off the stage. She tried to placate him, but he wasn't listening, he had his shirt out and kicked her too—right off the stage, across the hall and out through the exit.

Mr Sundri was never the same again. Years later, he convinced himself of his wife's infidelity. Had the serpent sneaked into his Garden of Eden?

Was he the base of the eternal triangle? Plagued by suspicion, he worked himself into a fit, packed his bags as if he were leaving home forever!

But he had a plan. He checked into a hotel overlooking his house just ten minutes later. Yes! He had a plan for sure. He spent a week there, never stirring out, like a peeping Tom, peering through a pair of binoculars at his own front door to see if the spoiler came around!

This time, he too got the third prize.

The crows and the mynahs fluttering around his home came in second and first!

Post script: In retrospect, sometimes Ruskin Bond and I wonder just *how* we could possibly have spent so many evenings in the Savoy bar. True, Nandu was a dear friend. That helped. He never let us ever pay for a drink. That helped. Though not entirely true that. We were old-fashioned enough to know that one does not accept hospitality if one was unable to make a return. So Ruskin would write the occasional story set in the hotel, chat up the odd customer, proof read the hotel menu for typos, or chat up the occasional hotel guests and fill them up on the stories about the hotel, while I would help Nandu with the odd and ends.

The dining room was empty. The neglected bar gradually resembled Miss Havisham's wedding cake; the threadbare curtains matched the moth-eaten carpet. The bartender stank to high heaven. If you mentioned this to him, he'd give you a withering look to say: '*Paani nahin hai hotel mein!*' (There's no water in the hotel!)

Even those charming Victorian love-seats where, once upon a time, lovers must have whispered sweet nothings to each other, succumbing to old age, gave up the ghost and sprouted springs that left dimples on the bottoms of those who had dared disturb their peace. The only bar-

decoration, apart from the clock that had stood still since the last Uttarkashi earthquake, was the tea filled five litre bottle of Johnny Walker Red Label Whisky, covered in algae and mildew, looking pale.

Occasionally, a lost shrew, with its weak eyesight, would complain, squealing at the lack of proper sustenance and head out through the door to the nearest eatery in Library. We did not have to do that. We'd taken the elementary precaution of buying our own boiled eggs, wrapped in old newsprint from the pavement stalls outside the gate. True, the newspaper had seen better days, but then so had the kitchen—in its present state, it was like a dungeon, tucked away from public view where on its greasy walls, yellowing calendars dating back to the Second Great War had unattended orders for roast chicken. The writing on the wall was clear and we could read it—it was time to move on.

Or was it that cocooned by its shell, we, all humble card-carrying member of the 'Friends of Nandu Club' felt as if we were reliving the days of the last Mughals?

Meanwhile, customer complaints mounted. One wrote: 'My fiancé and I booked a twin-bedded room,' she said, 'but we were given a double-bedded room. We hold you personally responsible for the fact that I find myself pregnant. Of course, none of this would have happened if you had given us the twin beds which we had originally booked!'

Near Bala Hisar, at Oakless, lived the late Rajmata Prithwi Bir Kaur of Jind. She bore a good deal of resemblance to her Romanian ancestors and had the lively spirit of those nomadic gypsies. 'Ah!' she would exclaim, remembering the past, 'I can hear the pitter-patter of the *rickshawala's* feet as they went past Oakless late at night on a rainy day.' She used to miss the good old days when there were parties and grand balls with dancing all night at Stifles, Hakman's and the Savoy. 'There used to be separate areas for the ladies with purdah—*not* like the trailer-trash you see today,' she'd say. The late HRH recalled: 'There was this man in a dinner jacket and bow tie, sitting a few tables away at a dance in the Hakman's Grand hotel. He was hitting the table with his thing, keeping time with the beat of the bongos!'

Nandu helpfully suggests: 'Wouldn't he have made less noise if it were folded?' She ignores the crude remark, lost in images of the past, adding: 'Anyway, a distracted waiter lost his balance, dropped the tray, and upturned a table almost rearranging the man's family jewels!' The late HRH used to divide her time between Delhi and the hills. 'I miss my golf up here,' she'd say, 'and the golf green is never too hot!'

As we chat, some drunks totter by on the road down below, workers from another construction sire—another hotel—coming up. She'd laugh, saying, 'Don't you worry, none of them will fall off the cliff. They won't let go of each other for fear if one falls—everyone will!'

'Pretty', as she was nicknamed, remained as pretty as she ever was. Around Oakless, she'd planted a host of trees, shrubs and *ringal*—the hill bamboo, to mask the view of the apartment blocks springing around her. Late His Highness Rajbir Singh of Jind loved his horses, dogs and had pet white mice, which he trained to do tricks in a mini-circus. They are all gone. Now, the greenery attracts the simians from the adjoining jungle that play havoc with the tin-roof. 'I don't know which is worse,' she'd say, 'the monkeys trying to get in or the ones trying to get out!'

As I get up to leave, the Scotsman in author Bill Aitken surfaces. He brings out his tartan kilt and begins to play the bagpipes. Slightly high, I tease him: 'What's worn under the kilt?' In his best Scottish accent, he replies: 'Nothing's worn under my kilt everything is workin' perfectly!' As we drop the latch on the massive gate, the royal insignia of the Maharajah of Jind is silhouetted against a fiery sunset for a fleeting moment.

There was a time when the hill station was a great place for flower shows and dog shows. The late HRH Rajmata Prithwi Bir Kaur of Jind's greyhounds, the pride of the Punjab, were reputedly 'as swift as birds', and the late Mahendra Kumari of Alwar's Great Danes—cropped ears, grey, blue and harlequins were traffic stoppers on the Mall. Of course Alsatians and German Shepherds of dubious descent found their way into the market to be mopped up by eager buyers. Into this grey market stepped enterprising Bhagwat, a school's night watchman. He loved dogs, about this there is no doubt. With great passion, he would round up every single stray puppy (and there was never a dearth of them!), give them a good shampoo, carry them in a neat wicker-basket to the steps outside Picture Palace and sell them to the unsuspecting as ferocious Bhutia pups.

Only time he got into a bit of a bother was when on one occasion, an irate customer took what he'd thought was a male puppy, but discovered weeks later that it was really a female!

If there were ever a true dog lover, he was one. And so was I. Over the years, our family has had many dogs—Cocker Spaniels, Labrador, Great Pyrenees and many, many mutts. The last adopted us—yet he had this terrible habit of going for long walkabouts which usually ended up in the *langar* (kitchen) of local police outpost.

Then, there was Mrs Roberts, who lived some ways up the road from us, two kilometres away from the nearest bazaar—who took in any stray that happened to go by her cottage. She had them for the sole reason that she loved them.

Long, long ago, she and her husband were the toast of the hill station, wined and dined by the glitterati; they'd dance the nights away in the ballrooms of our little town. Then, one dark morning Mr Roberts passed away, suddenly, while collecting his war pension, leaving Mrs Roberts alone to fend for herself. A couple of unpleasant encounters later, she turned her back on the human race to retreat within her garden gate in Cosy Nook.

For some twenty years and more, no one ever saw her again, except the local vendors who'd leave food at her doorstep and once a month, find a cheque pinned to the door. This carried on for years till one day she too passed on to the everglades.

How did folks find out? A chorus of howling reverberated eerily that moonlit night. What happened to the dogs? Some were taken in adoption by residents on our hillside as they scampered all over our hill station; others, escaped into the adjoining villages where their descendants, or so I'm told, roam around to this day.

Today, if you see any strange looking strays wandering around—short legs, shorter hair and no tails—rest assured it's a part of our tradition when *gupp* has finally met gossip. For in some sequestered corner of the hill station, someone's pedigreed basset hounds have been playing footsie with the milkman's home-reared bhotia!

Chapter 12

Serving Spirits

Hajar gagriko much banda garna sakincha,
ek manisko much banda garna sakina
NEPALI PROVERB

(The mouth of a thousand pitchers can be closed
but not one man's mouth.)

One has often been asked why spirits are partial to the hills. Inexplicably, denizens of the other world seem to fill up the sleepy hollows, especially at night when the rest of the citizenry have gone to sleep. Why is it that only we have haunted dak bungalows, graveyards, cottages, houses and forests? Is it because of our well-preserved cemeteries?

The answer perhaps lies in a bit of each. Every cottage retains its own character. The older it gets, the stronger the pull of the past. Folks have lived and loved and passed away under its roof. Stand in the shady veranda, brush the walls and you can almost hear the words spoken in these rooms. The furniture has tales to tell. The mirror hides images of long gone residents who crossed this threshold many, many years ago. Vibrations from the past linger to reveal themselves at will. And the tin-roofs creak and groan with changes in temperature like in the old Cantonment Office, set up in 1827, on a spur below Char Dukan, where a long time ago you would have found my father working late into the night.

Ram Singh, the greying watchman was convinced the office was haunted by a ghostly spectre accompanied by his pack of phantom dogs.

'The sound of someone scampering down the roof would make you rush outside!' he'd tell my father. 'But if you stepped out to look—nothing—except the breeze soughing through the deodar trees late at night.'

Near the forest, was the Old Theatre, opposite the Guard Room where the sentry's unfailing cry of: *'Hu-kam-dar?'* (Who comes there?) would freeze any intruder in his tracks. Everyone knew that the warning was uttered only thrice; after which, if unheeded, the redcoats would open fire.

Many years ago, a ghostly black spaniel would enter the sentry room as soon as the lamp was lit at sundown. He was gentle, but not overtly friendly. After hanging around all night, he would disappear at dawn. Though, while the canine was around, something in his bristling demeanour ensured that the normally bad-mouthed soldiers would be on best behaviour, going out in pairs, and careful not to use any foul language.

All went well till one night, one of the troopers who having drunk a drop too many struck out on his own and made a fatal mistake by using a swear word. By next morning he was lisping, and soon after his speech was gone. By dusk he was delirious and that very night he went into shock and died.

Our phantom spaniel vanished. Who knows if he had in some way been responsible for the death of the drunken guard?

Drinking though is certainly not one of Bhoot Aunty's (who's been so named by the taxi-drivers plying this road) problems. 'She's the lost soul of a young bride who was killed in a car that went over the side on a stormy night,' the driver tells me. Others say she survived the wreck, indeed being the first one to be rescued from the mangled heap at the bottom of the ravine. They brought her up but left her alone on the roadside as the rescuers hurried back to help the others. Maybe the shock of standing alone in thunder, lightning and rain prove too much for her weak heart? Who knows?'

'If you see her, avoid looking into her baleful eyes, just drive past. Don't even *think* of giving her a lift!' He shudders at the thought. 'There's a good chance, she'll personally escort you to the bottom of the hill,' he says.

No such chaperone for the late night visitor who finds a friendly dog of non-descript origin, attach itself to you, as it lags behind on the long haul to the top of the hill as one goes past the Cobbler's Perch, where those incredible craftsmen of yore once plied their trade making belts, saddles and shoes for the soldiers who peopled this area.

A hundred years later, on moonlit nights you will still hear the ring of hammers beating pliable leather on awls or is it the thumping of your heart as it tries to jump into your mouth. By the time you sort it all out, the dog has vanished into thin air. Not a trace of him till you meet him again, another night on the same road.

Far away lies in wait, the famed *churail* or witch of Park Estate, whose feet always face backwards—she will trail you at the dead of night. She is the spirit of one of those denied a proper funeral and while you may not see her, the footsteps are distinct and audible. Do not be surprised if she catches up with you, accosts you or even speaks to you. Its only when you try to run away that she takes great delight in pelting stones or hurling large boulders after you as you scamper downhill.

Beware! If she catches up with you on the run as it were, she'll hurl you on your back, and maul like a wild cat gone rabid!

These and other tales of haunting fill up the lonely cottages atop the hill like the grand mansion, where on moonlit nights the owners were roused from their slumber to find their shoes being thrown around, pictures falling off the walls and cushions being flung across the room. When they bolted out of the house, across the yard, through the trees and down the narrow Eyebrow path, they walked straight into the unhappy spectre of an Englishman who had murdered his young wife, wrongly suspecting her of infidelity.

Often, he appears out of nowhere, wringing his hands in grief, startling late evening walkers as he shuffles off trying to undo what can no longer be undone.

Should you see three little children—two boys and a girl riding the seesaw in the park at Char Dukan after the lights have come on in the nearby Church, please just let them be! They mean no harm and turn up on the little flat once a year on the very same day those three infants drowned in an unprotected pool at a nearby cottage.

After the accident, the owners simply filled up the pond with gravel to erase all memories of the tragedy. Forgotten by Time, in an increasingly crowded town, the three apparitions have nowhere else to go.

Other residents will tell you of the spirits in the bamboo clusters found swaying in the breeze in Bansagadh, on the other side of Hathipaon, where forty years ago, a hunter chasing his quarry—a marauding black bear—mistakenly shot a woman cutting grass, screened from view by the thicket. Sometimes on windy nights, her ghost returns looking for the bundle of hay she left behind on that fatal day. Fodder in the hills can often be more precious than life.

'And life means nothing to the *momiai*,' my mother used to tell me. 'Once these ghostly bands of man-hunters commence their activities they stop for nothing.'

Momiai is an old superstition about a magic unguent which confers invulnerability against all weapons, and which is unrivalled for the quick healing of wounds. Trouble is it is extracted from the human cranium.

In 1938, a teacher and old-time resident, Jim Keelan narrated the story he had heard from Hans Ram, the village chief of Gaonkhet: 'There is a class of men whose whole business is to collect this *momiai;* and these we all call *momiaiwallahi*. They are a brutal and an unscrupulous lot, who frequent lonely roads on the lookout for solitary travellers. They carry long staves, the ends of which secrete certain essences which, if a man smells, it will immediately deprive him of his rightful senses.'

'If by chance a traveller comes their way, they by some trick or stratagem, beguile him into smelling the rod. Instantly, his senses forsake him, and the devil leads him away into the jungle where accomplices await their arrival. Having arrived at the appointed spot, the victim is bound and strung up by the heels, with his head over a cauldron.'

'Beneath the cauldron, they quickly light a big fire. When these preparations are complete, they knock a hole in the victim's head, whereupon the *momiai* trickles out, drop by drop, and collects in the vessel below.'

'Afterwards the body of the man is buried, and all traces of the deed carefully effaced, so that thereafter never a trace of the traveller may be found.'

And in winter, few travellers could be found up here in the 1960s, when older folk from the hills would lock-up their homes in November to winter in the valley down below. Our neighbour, Mrs Edith Walsh ran a guest house at Wolfsburn, her cottage on the hill. She'd head down the hill leaving the place in the care of her loyal caretaker, Kalyan Singh. One year, on a cold winter's night, aged ninety years, she quietly slipped away to the land of eternal rainbows. Or so we believed till the night, the caretaker, dusty, crumpled, dishevelled, pale as a sheet, almost knocked our door down at daybreak.

'Saili sahib! Saili sahib!' the words tumbled out of his mouth, jostling and bumping into one another in a frantic haste to get spoken. Breathlessly, he managed to stutter to my father: 'She's back! It's March and she's back! Walsh memsahib kept me up all of last night!'

Apparently, she kept rattling the old chain on the outhouse door! She kept saying: 'Kalyan Singh, *darwaza kholo!* Kalyan Singh *darwaza kholo*!' (Open the door! Open the door!). We never saw the old chowkidar again. Kalyan Singh ran away to his mountain home, breathing fear instead of air, and vanished forever!

Somehow, one person who was doing no vanishing was Gopal Sharma, a mild-mannered, quiet, office clerk in one of our forgotten schools on the fringes of town, who usually kept his opinions to himself. One evening he startled everyone by suddenly chirping up in the voice of a woman!

Apparently, a spirit had taken possession of his body. Mass hysteria ensued. In the girl's dorms, the students started speaking in tongues. Pundits from far were brought in by the school's owners to exorcise the demons. They advised special prayers with fire-worship to chase the devils away.

'I was in a car with three boys,' Gopal said, in a girl's voice, wailing: 'We took the wrong road and got lost!'

'Turn the car around! yelled Rahul. Instead the driver backed the car into the *khud*, killing all of us! Now we're stuck in limbo!' The voice pleaded: 'Please! Help us get release from this!'

All the religious rituals were done dutifully and iron stakes were hammered into the four corners of all the school buildings. At the time of writing, peace reigns. But wait until dark. A hush descends upon the campus, not a leaf stirs on the trees, nothing else dares move. It is as if they too are waiting for the spirits to leave.

Last week, I received a letter from the late Stephen Cohen, whose parents in the 1950s, worked in one of our schools. He writes, 'I used to have a room all by myself that overlooked the Dun valley. It was just awesome, especially in the old days when there was no smog in the clear summer months, and the moon rose over the dorms. Our dog Kim used to howl his head off even though he was not afraid of other animals; perhaps he was sensing something just as I did when mom and dad left me alone if they went to town or Dehra.'

And he remembers: 'One day in winter, when the school had gone for the Christmas holidays in the late evening, I was surrounded with the cloying scent of *Ittar* and in the dead of winter, there were no flowers in the garden. But I carried the smell of roses all the way from the boys school shed till I reached the doors of home. The bearer put his hand over my mouth and told me not to say anything as I spoke to him. Years later, he told mom, that there was a fight for my soul between the good spirits and the bad. I was lucky that the good ones triumphed as the *djinns* celebrated their victory by a liberal sprinkling of *Ittar*.'

'In 1950, we had just come to the new school, where mom worked in the junior section. On a rainy night, with mist swirling all around, she saw a very regal looking man soaked to the bone, standing in his dinner jacket at the end of the junior school flats, near the steps. She was just going to ask him if he needed to walk under her umbrella, when she looked down for a second to avoid a puddle and he had disappeared.'

A few days ago, Mr RH, a regular visitor who is given to his early morning walks around the hill, told me that as he rounded a corner past one of our older guest houses, he heard a group of ashen-faced tourists anxious to settle their bill and leave.

'Couldn't sleep a wink last night!' they told the manager, adding: 'This young English memsahib and her wailing kids kept knocking on the windows all night.'

'But there's no such woman staying with us,' protested the harried man.

'That's exactly why we are leaving!' They whispered, paid their bill upfront, scurried out to the waiting taxis, never to come back again.

Among our ethereal dwellers, the playful ghosts at an abandoned school, along the old Oak Road, make merry at night, on the swings in the playground. On moonlit nights, people lose their nerve at the sight of empty swings swaying wildly.

'Don't ever touch those swings at night!' the night watchman warned me. 'I did and was taken for the ride of my life!'

I guess you too could go for the ride of your life if you go past the dilapidated building near Douglas Dale spring after the sun has set. Here, a lovely lady in white waits forlornly at the gate at night. Let me warn you, simply walk past. To this day, no one knows who she is, or for whom she waits.

And then there's Camel's Back Road—once a favourite tryst for lovers. This too used to have a fair sprinkling of ghosts, till modern day God-men moved their summer headquarters there. Wisely, the fearful ghosts have all fled.

It was in 1967 that I first heard my friends gossip of a young man in our midst who wanted to be a writer.

'He sleeps during the day and writes all night,' or so went the *gupp*.

'You mean a phantom in our midst like the ghost who walks all night!' I joked.

But the joke was on me.

Six decades later, author Ruskin Bond continues to write, faster and more furiously than ever. I believe he could wrap up many more books but for all the kind help he gets from his fans. They return again and again to end up clogging his threshold. At times they miss his second floor entrance to Ivy Cottage, and arrive literally at the room on the roof only to realise that it has been over sixty years since he actually first lived in and wrote *The Room on the Roof*.

Our present day arrival's must-do list includes Kempty Falls, Lal Tibba and author Ruskin Bond! How they test his patience! Especially when aroused like a bear from his siesta as fond tourists arrive at Ivy Cottage waiting for him to bless their honeymoon, their children or get photographed in the middle of the afternoon. Never mind even if he is still in his pyjamas!

At noon one day, there was a knock on the door. Ruskin opened the door to let in an out-of-breath senior citizen who promptly proceeded to plonk himself on the sofa.

'Get me a glass of water.' he ordered Ruskin. Ruskin obliged.

'Now call the sahib!' he brusquely said.

By now Ruskin realised that the fellow had not recognised him, so he said: '*Sahib bahar gaya hai*!' (Sahib has gone out!).

'Oh ho! And I have come all this way,' grumbled the old man, fumbling in his pockets, fishing out a ten rupee note which he shoved into Ruskin's shirt pocket as a tip. He left saying: 'Tell him, I had come.'

'I saw him waddling down the road without even a backward glance!' remembers Ruskin. As I get ready to leave, some bright-eyed entrepreneurs arrive. Their request is unique—they'd like to name their proposed school after him.

'How wonderful!' he said, then baulked for they wanted to name it the St Ruskin Bond Memorial School.

He had a hard time dissuading them.

'After all I'm still alive and well,' he tells me. 'Luckily for me they settled for St Dreamy Valley High School instead.'

Arriving for lunch at a hotel in Barlowganj, an effusive government official greeted him saying: 'Sir! I have always been a fan of yours. What great books: *The Man-eater of Rudraprayag* and *The Man-eaters of Kumaon!*'

'Yes!' Ruskin mumbled as he shuffled off, adding: 'Jim Corbett would have been pleased to hear that.'

Once, as I got up to leave, a retired Major-General announced his arrival by booming: 'I have brought you a present!' as he shook the author's hand furiously.

'Ah!' Ruskin and I presume, 'Here comes a bottle of good old army rum!' We ask him to sit down and be comfortable.

With a regal flourish, out pop two volumes of his memoirs, handsomely bound in leather.

'Get it reviewed in *Outlook, India Today* or *Time Magazine*,' he barks, adding: 'You must know all the editors there!'

Ruskin manages a smile, promises to do his best.

Six months later the books were still there, no use for the stove to keep warm but great—as door-stoppers.

Yet some things never change.

Like that streak of fiery crimson across the distant horizon. It's our famed winter line, a spectacular sunset best seen from the ridge or some of the higher points of the hill station in the fall. If you wake up early, you can witness the same effect in the eastern sky, before sunrise.

Ah! Another day full of *gupp* and gossip dawns. Time to go back to the bazaar again!

Thanks

A great many people have inspired this book.

To Bikash Niyogi, my Publisher, for not taking too long to say 'Yes'.

To my dear friends: Bhanwar Sa'ab, Chunu bhai, Cyril Sahib, John, Misraji, Nandu, Victor and Maya. They all know gossip, not truth, makes our world go round. Try denying a rumour and it'll be hanging around like a lost puppy.

To Prannoy and Radhika, avowed believers in public opinion, they prefer leaving the *gupps* to me.

To my biggest critics, the women in my life: my daughters, Tulika & Tania; Nia and Ria my grandchildren and Abha, my generous long-suffering wife. Come to think of it, what could I possibly have done without my pets Kaali and Bhuri!

To my friend, the venerable Ruskin Bond, who prodded me on: 'Come on with your *gupp-shupp*?'

To TK Manoj Kumar for the sketches. Gattu for his advice in all matters big and small.

To my editor Supriya for applying her special skills and Ritu Topa for the design.

To Prerna for keeping my desk together. And to those who have not been mentioned here, you chatter-boxes never looked for praise, but I want you too to know that I appreciate your help. You know who you are. Go ahead. Discover your contributions as the gossip unfolds.

I promise this is no *gupp*!